THE MASTER MASON

יהוה

THE
MASTER
MASON

THE REASON OF BEING

A
TREATISE
ON THE
THIRD DEGREE
OF
FREEMASONRY

by
A Brother of the Hermetic Art
❖ *Gregory* ❖ *B.* ❖ *Stewart* ❖

A.L. 6017

Other works by the author:
Masonic Traveler, FreemasonInformation.com (online)
What is Freemasonry, ebook (online)
Masonic Traveler — Essays and Commentary (print)
The Apprentice — The World and the Universe As One (print)
Fellow of the Craft — By Wisdom a House is Built (print)

The Master Mason
The Reason of Being
A Treatise on the Third Degree of Freemasonry

by Gregory B. Stewart

Copyright ©2017, FmI Publishing
ISBN-13: 978-0-9862041-2-8
ISBN-10: 0-9862041-2-9
Library of Congress PCN 2017916767

First Printing

Published by FmI Publishing
P.O. Box 16441
Los Angeles, CA 91316

Online: www.FreemasonInformation.com
Email: masonictraveler@gmail.com

Questions, comments, inquiries — please send correspondence to the email or address above.

Words, Art and Design by Gregory Stewart, 2011-2017

Edited by Kyle Robert Beswick

Dedicated
to
Those in Pursuit
of the
Hermetic Art

MM
XVII

⁜ L ⁜ V ⁜ X ⁜

Thank you to the following people whom, without their support, this book would not have been published:

Gene and Angela Ammerman, Boise Lodge, No. 2, A.F. & A.M.; Ariel Añaza, 33°; Johnny Arias, 32°, South Pasadena Masonic Temple, No. 290; Daniel C. Barston; Kirk J. Bielskis; Daniel Bjorklund, Enlightenment Lodge, No. 198; Jonathan Carr, Brookwood Lodge, No. 509, Brookwood, AL; Andrew Chellinsky; Stephen Consello, Past Master, St. John's Lodge, No. 115; Chris Davis, Corinthian Lodge, No. 230; Gordon Echlin, St. John's, No. 63; Luis Farinha; Luis A. Feliciano; Carlos (Caly) Fiallos, Muskoka Lodge, No. 360, GLCPO; William Foley, Apollo-King Solomon's Lodge, No. 13, NY; Nathan Miller Foster; Matt Frye, Glen Burnie Lodge, No. 213, A.F. & A. M.; Mike Garrett; Jade D. Gibbon, PM, Lakewood Lodge, No. 170; Nick Hayworth, PM, Island City Lodge, No. 215, Alameda, CA; William ES Hearnshaw, Cockfosters Lodge, No 6883, UGLE; Keith Inchierca; Gary Iverson, Whittier RAM, No. 91; Jeffrey S. Kupperman; June E. Lennon, Master Mason; Luxamore; Electric Maenad — Self-Made Mutant Cabal; Kevin P. Menard, PhD; John Merrick; Bro. Tim Parker-Smith, St Aldhelm's Lodge, No.2559, UGLE; David L. Pearson, Kirkland Lodge, No. 150, Kirkland, WA, and Liberal Arts Lodge, No. 677, Los Angeles, CA; Gar Pickering; Edward Poplawski; Bro. Nickolas Robinson, Island City Lodge, No. 215, Alameda, CA; Bro. N.S. Jack Ruby, Eureka North Warren Lodge, No. 594; Gustavus Schlichting, Sanilac Lodge, No. 237; Geoffrey B. Schumann, Culver City Foshay, No.

467, F. & A. M.; Scott A. Schwartzberg, Boynton Lodge, No. 236, Grand Lodge of Florida; Prenna Sergent; W. Bro. Andrew Smith; Hal Sparks; Caleb Thomas, Anchorage Lodge, No. 17; Bro. Alex Towey; Toby Vanderbeek; Nicholas Vettese, St John's Lodge, No. 115, Philadelphia; Anthony Ward, Luftbrücke Lodge, No. 838; Matthew Weedmark, St. John's, No. 63, Carleton Place, ON, Canada; Craig Whitaker, Tazewell, TN; Ann Arbor-Fraternity Lodge, No. 262, Grand Lodge of Michigan; ChewBeardca; Conclave Arcanum and Jewel P. Lightfoot Lodge, No. 1283.

A very special thanks to Jorge Dagang and Shawn Michael.

For D. S.
my
everything...

and to K. S. and N. S.
my past, present
and future.

ILLUSTRATIONS

*Illustrated by the author

CONTENTS

ANIMA MUNDI - THE JOURNEY THROUGH YESOD
GREGORY B. STEWART, PEN AND INK
2017

PREFACE

Warriors and Priests

Once upon a time, someone said to me after a Scottish Rite meeting that Freemasonry (and the Rite) can only exist with an equal balance of warriors and priests. I thought I understood what that meant at the time, but it wasn't until 10 years on that it made sense to me. Warriors and priests. Obviously, the warriors exist to enforce the dogma — the rote ritual and institutional memory — and the priests to interpret its meaning, knowingly or unknowingly to craft the subtext in the body of the work. Neither more important than the other, yet both thinking they alone are the beating heart of the institution (and consequently, the part that matters).

I pen these thoughts in a season out of sequence from its predecessors in this trilogy about the symbolic lodge. I won't burden you with the details of managing life's priorities, but taking this sabbatical has given me the space to reflect on the words herein. This work represents a culmination of sorts, in both a literal sense and in a metaphoric one, as we reach the zenith of lodge masonry and the journey of "our" work. I say our work because this has been an undertaking together in becoming a priest of Freemasonry.

Let me first address the formalities of this work, *The Master Mason*.

In your hands is a formal exploration of the symbolism and allegory at work in the third degree of (Scottish Rite) Freemasonry. I include the SR implication because as the *Webb-Preston* ritual in practice today seems to be devoid of many of the deeper symbolic and esoteric underpinnings that once graced some forms of blue lodge practice. *The result of the warriors being in charge too long, perhaps.* So then, through that lens, this work seeks to find the hidden esoteric connections and find sense in their relationship with the centuries-old ritual that crowns the process of becoming a Freemason. As with its predecessors, *The Apprentice* and *Fellow of the Craft*, this work seeks to find parallel with its esoteric siblings through the Golden Dawn, numerology, tarot, the Kabbalah and a few other traditions that call the arcane and occult world their home. Which brings us back to the analogy of warriors and the priests.

It would be impossible to say when I found myself a priest of Freemasonry and no longer concerned with the letter or execution of the law (ritual). I found that the spirit of the warrior left me to find its fight in another day. It was in this transition that I came to embrace the "deeper meaning of Freemasonry" and strive to interpret what was hidden in the subtext of the work, finding which parts of it resonated most deeply within me. This meandering path took me through a host of "esoteric" traditions that at one point or another found favor (and discontent) in the practice of contemporary Freemasonry. It has been the course of that journey that has found its way into this exploration on the symbolic lodge, and in particular the becoming of a true Master.

From my explorations, the one steady drum-beat that continues to pulse within my chest is that of the blazingly bright connections to the *Hermetica* — if not in the literal word then in the unflinching spirit of what is being communicated. Freemasonry is, at its heart, an initiatic system that has a distinct beginning, middle and end from which a new beginning starts anew. It's in this spirit of renewal, in part, that the whole process has an almost reincarnational feel to it. You're born, you mature and then your old self ceases to exist as you undergo a transformation (much in the same way you experience becoming an apprentice mason). So then, Freemasonry is cyclical. It is a self-contained system that propagates itself (in a manner) and converts those who enter into it into something wholly new and reborn. This, then, is the achievement of mastery. But, is that all there is to it?

One of the great lessons from this experience is that of synchronicity — that in-the-moment-ness that you feel after you've slipped from that headspace and realize you are no longer in it. Perhaps it's a trance, or an altered state of being or even a deeply meditative state. However you quantify it, it is this state of being that becoming a master entails. Interestingly, this makes for a unique description of the state of mastery — it does little to truly say what the grist of being a Master entails. The masonic ritual takes great strides to impart this grit, but this is only one moment of an otherwise long life filled with similar moments.

Because of this eternal bombardment of moments, the one constant we can bring to bear is how we choose to approach them. Are we applying our self-mastery or are we allowing our base nature to dictate our thoughts and actions? This is at the heart of ALL of these religious and esoteric traditions by encouraging us to find and operate our inner mastery and elevate above the fray. Ironically, this is exactly the transformation from a warrior into a priest.

Pike writes, "The Priesthood, custodian of Faith, wholly rests upon this basis of knowledge, and it is in its teachings we must recognize the Divine Principle of the Eternal Word." It's interesting in that this seems an amalgam of both priest and warrior by holding fast the "eternal word." Perhaps, like that elusive state of synchronicity, mastery is a state of flux forever ebbing and flowing through the morals and dogmas at work in the being of a Freemason.

And yet, here still we sit contemplating what it means to be a Master. In *Fellow of the Craft,* one of the conclusions it explored was the historical basis that being a master was, at one time, the pinnacle of the system. Once a fellow, the only next step was to become a Master of a lodge (as we see in the Holy Royal Arch working). That mastership was a rite reserved for only a few who sought to lead and thus were granted this peculiar title. Can one, truly, claim to be a Master, or is it a title bestowed by others in recognition of one's work? Perhaps that is the heart of it, the mere asking of the question — "what is a Master?" — that allows us to philosophically claim that title. Here again, the priest becomes the warrior only to become the priest again.

Such a confluence of states of being. Warrior/ Priest, Fellow/Master, in the moment/not in the moment. This is the complexity of unraveling the becoming of a Master Mason. It is this confluence of states that gives us a foundation from which to turn speculation into operation — a theme whose current emanates and returns through the allegorical *Sefirot of Yesod*, which is one of the explorations in this work. Perhaps we can only conclude that mastery is only a periodic state of achievement, one that reveals itself slowly over time and in stages as we evolve in our states of consciousness.

At the very start of the Master's degree in *Morals and Dogma*, Pike writes, *"To understand literally the symbols and allegories of Oriental books as to ante-historical matters, is willfully to close our eyes against the Light. To translate the symbols into the trivial and commonplace, is the blundering of mediocrity."*

Here in, then, is an attempt towards becoming a warrior priest, stepping into that light and translating the master's symbols into something meaningful and rarified.

Fiat LvX

Greg Stewart
Los Angeles, California
Autumn, A.L. 6017

FREEMASONRY DEFINED

An explanation for those new to the fraternity

Freemasonry is a post-collegiate male fraternity dedicated to the spiritual development of the initiate into a broader sense of the self, how he relates to the Divine, and his contributory role in the world. It conveys this message through a series of progressive degrees initiating the candidate into a deeper level of understanding and membership. Ultimately, the raised Master Mason is given the allegorical tools to further work on and develop his Masonic intuition.

The largest and oldest fraternal order in the world, Freemasonry crosses all religious boundaries to bring together its adherents of all countries, sects, and opinion in peace and harmony to work towards the betterment of all mankind. A universal brotherhood, Freemasonry is dedicated to serving the divine through service to family, country, and humankind.

Freemasonry is a philosophical organization emphasizing the study of moral symbols to build character in its participants. This education is, in part, the foundation of a more profound understanding of mankind and his existence in society.

SCOTTISH RITE FREEMASONRY

The college of Freemasonry, the Scottish Rite presents the advanced degrees of Freemasonry beyond that of the third degree or Master Mason. Scottish Rite Freemasonry degrees are further education on the principals of the Craft Lodge with their own perspective of the three principal degrees in the lodge of perfection.

Scottish Rite Freemasonry is a compelling and conquering spiritual force, the reasons of which are revealed in the degrees.

A common definition of the society says,

"Scottish Freemasonry is the foe of intolerance, fanaticism, and superstition. It battles every form of racial and sectarian prejudice and bigotry. It is a mighty exponent of freedom in thought, religion, and government. Thus, the Scottish Rite is a rite of instruction. It interprets the symbols and allegories of Masonry in the light of history and philosophy using the words of the supreme prophets of humanity, ceremonies of the great religions of the world, and significant episodes from history to point the moral and adorn the tale."

THE SYMBOLIC LODGE

More metaphoric than tangible, the Symbolic Lodge is a collective term for the first three ceremonies of Freemasonry. Consisting of the Apprentice, Fellowcraft and Master Masons degrees, the symbolic lodge is the entry point of Freemasonry and its concordant degrees in the Scottish Rite tradition. Craft, or Blue Lodge Masonry, are other terms that can be used interchangeably with the idea of the Symbolic Lodge.

In the Scottish Rite, the Symbolic Lodge is the first three degrees not practiced in the conveyance of the Rite system, deferring instead to the more localized practice of Grand Lodge Masonry. Different from the mainstream system, the Scottish Rite progression differs in that the Hiramic legend does not reach its culmination after the third-degree ceremony, instead allowing it to continue in a more organic progression — bringing new implications and insight.

Applying an esoteric understanding of the Symbolic Lodge, the first, second and third degree represents the first (or last) three steps in the Kabbalistic Tree of Life, beginning at the Sefirot of Malkuth, moving up the pillar of wisdom onto the path of Tav, completing the journey at the Sefirot of Yesod. Taken in this configuration, the foundation, or root, of the tree is made secure through the material world out of the existential chaos of ain soph — which is the world around us.

MASTER

As a noun, from the late Old English mægester "one having control or authority," from Latin magister (n.) "chief, head, director, teacher" (source of Old French maistre, French maître, Spanish and Italian maestro, Portuguese mestre, Dutch meester, German Meister), contrastive adjective ("he who is greater") from magis (adv.) "more," from PIE *mag-yos-, *comparative of root meg- "great."*

Form influenced in Middle English by Old French cognate maistre. Meaning "original of a recording" is from 1904. In academic senses (from Medieval Latin magister) it is attested from late 14c., originally a degree conveying authority to teach in the universities. As an adjective from late 12c.

meg

Proto-Indo-European root meaning "great." It forms all or part of: acromegaly; Almagest; Charlemagne; maestro; magisterial; magistral;

magistrate; Magna Carta; magnate; magnitude; magnum; magnanimity; magnanimous; magni-; Magnificat; magnificence; magnificent; magnify; magniloquence; magniloquent; Magnus; maharajah; maharishi; mahatma; Mahayana; Maia; majesty; major; major-domo; majority; majuscule; master; maxim; maximum; May; mayor; mega-; megalo-; mickle; Mister; mistral; mistress; much; omega.

It is the hypothetical source of Armenian mets "great;" Sanskrit mahat- "great, mazah- "greatness;" Avestan mazant- "great;" Hittite mekkish "great, large;" Greek megas "great, large;" Latin magnus "great, large, much, abundant," major "greater," maximus "greatest;" Middle Irish mag, maignech "great, large;" Middle Welsh meith "long, great." Avestan mazant- "great;" Hittite mekkish "great, large;" Greek megas "great, large;" Latin magnus "great, large, much, abundant," major "greater," maximus "greatest;" Middle Irish mag, maignech "great, large;" Middle Welsh meith "long, great."

Online Etymology Dictionary

Old French and Old Latin:

to acquire complete knowledge.

In Masonic parlance, a Master is:
A person with the ability or power to use, control, or dispose of something.

A person eminently skilled in something, as an occupation, art, or science.

A person whose teachings others accept or follow.

A worker qualified to teach apprentices and to carry on a trade independently.

A Master Mason is the personification of GMHB.

The teachings of these readings are not
sacramental, so far as they go beyond
the realm of morality into those
of other domains of
Thought and
Truth

PHASE

Illustrated illusions trace at the edge
Probing, curious, faint.

Gently, like a dwindling embrace,
it comes.

Suffocatingly sublime, distant,
cold, empty and vast.

Indigo and violet is a riot,
sounds turned color,
of sleep, eternity, despair, and fear.

One by one, the host of heaven,
opens to the eyes.
Silent observers to oblivion.

Veil between is laid like a shroud.
Arrow assailing the margin.
A sign of the hunt begins anew.

Her vesper escaping.
On invisible breath.

Rain of twilight baths us,
drowning the joyous rain of,
unquenchable fire.

Hecate crawls, slowly with poise,
        her eye wide, glaring,
                gazing as it climbs upwards.

Streaked and scarred, safe and comforting.
        She sees without seeing,
                boiling in its cold glow.

Yesod has arisen, again and again,
        Forever the same, but always again.

In darkness it seeps, drowned in its radiance.
        Resplendent in the memory of her husband.
                Chasing and forlorn,
                        Rebirthed to remind us
                                of the balance between.

Stranger in the eyes of heaven,
        reflecting HIS glory,
                guardian of its gaze.

Calm is the passage.
        Silent unyielding its softness.
                To its last faint sliver,
                        gone again,
                                with the dawn.

ZIGGURAT

Steppes lost in shrouding mist,
        A lone illumination on the ecliptic.

Edges, sharp and true,
        the blocks square,
                show not a makers mark.

Steppes rise, lost in the shrouding mist,
        braziers aglow, air alight,
                hissing, burning the spirits.

Silent, alone,
        imposing it opens,
                only for the worthy.

Admitted on desire,
Passed on quality.
The steppes rising,
        raise, risen,
                arise.

The light atop the stone,
        extinguished.
                Embers and ash,
                        Deep in the builders repose.
From heats final wave,
        a star remembers its birth,
                senses its reawakening.

Decay shrouds what was living,
Stones sing to stone,
its chorus of silence.

Weight crushes in,
cut stone stacked in order and measure,
giving way to mountain.

Form is no more.
Mother mountain births sun.
Blackness swaddles the seed.
Seed stirs and shoots.
Arise. Rise. Risen.

On high the steppes,
push towards heaven's gaze.
Through the mist becoming the glow.

Child of mountain,
babe of widow.

Was, now, shall be.
To become, we are from.
To be, we become.

Joining the chorus of stone
to the cosmos.

MASTER

I am dust made real by desire,
wet and naked in wind and storm

Shadow shaped but formless,
twisted, molded and torn.

By declaration, I breathe life,
into what has been created,

bound on edge by air and fire,

a force of will alone.

Nature is the great Teacher of man;
for it is the Revelation of God.

ALBERT PIKE
MORALS & DOGMA
THE APPRENTICE DEGREE

————————————

So much has been done, exclaimed the soul of
Frankenstein — more, far more, will I achieve: treading
in the steps already marked, I will pioneer a new way,
explore unknown powers, and unfold to the world the
deepest mysteries of creation.

MARY SHELLEY
FRANKENSTEIN
VOLUME I, CHAPTER 3

THE MASTER MASON

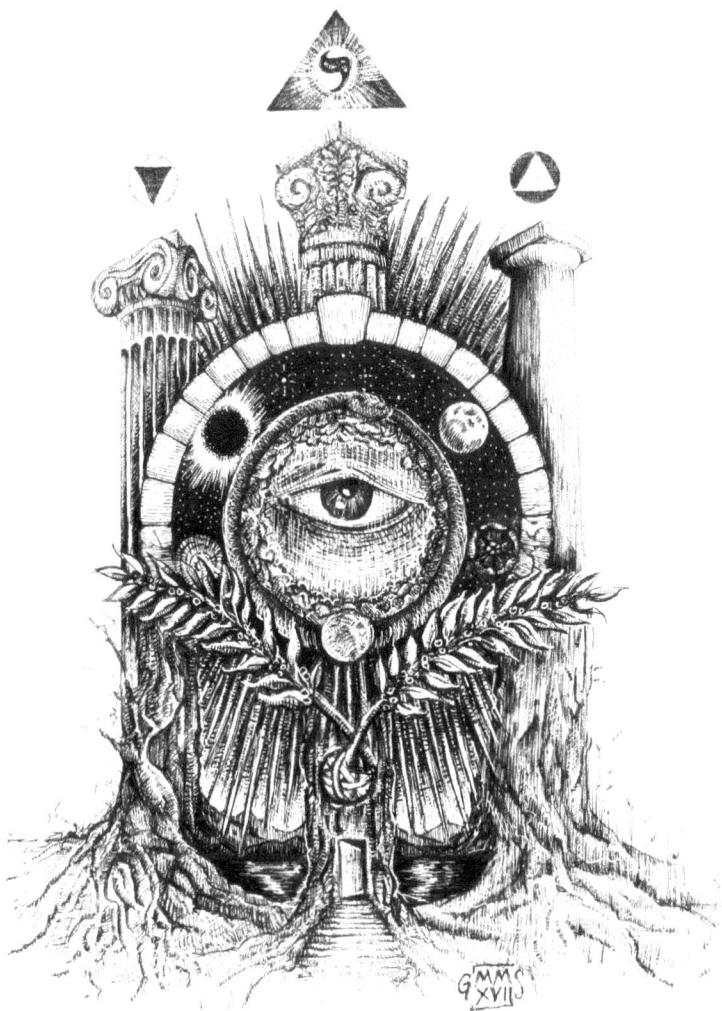

THE TREE OF LIFE
GREGORY STEWART, PEN & INK ON BOARD
2017

To the power of the cosmos, which we address in silence,
allow me to accept the weight of our pure speech offering
from the heart and soul that it reaches up to you.

Grant me my request to not fail
in absorbing the knowledge that benefits my essence;
give me power from wisdom so that I may
enlighten those who have ears to hear
and mind to accept.

Allow me to advance in Life and Light
and further the Great Work
in sanctification with
the All.

Every true Mason has come into the realization that there is but one Lodge — that is, the Universe — and but one Brotherhood, composed of everything that moves or exists in any of the planes of Nature.

MANLY P HALL
THE LOST KEYS OF FREEMASONRY

THE SYMBOLIC LODGE

At long last you have reached the threshold of the third degree. This cycle of the Symbolic Lodge culminates at this degree as the outcome of the journey up Jacob's ladder, over the three steps of maturity, through the path of the five orders of architecture, and up the seven steps of the liberal arts and sciences reaching the zenith of that progression at the east gate which is our destruction, of which we are now to enjoy as the outcome of our work as an Apprentice and Fellow of the Craft. We are now, by degree, a Master of the Craft — eligible to receive all of its rights and benefits. Yet, as we shall find in this degree, our life as a Freemason exists within the context of the second degree, as our work is continuous and never fulfilled, remaining a lifelong quest towards perfection. This quest is a journey towards the divine and is, the Hermetic texts suggest, the quest for beauty — which stems from the essential and ever-present manifestation of the divine creation. Here we stand: across the porch of temple, atop the fifteen steps and over the threshold, which is the third degree. What awaits beyond the portal is unlike anything experienced thus far in our journey; it is the pivotal point in our journey as we move from duality in the second degree to the elevation in symbolic assumption, into a third position that gives us balance for the work ahead. As two represents a perfect division, three is the form of a perfect balance as opposition becomes perfection. This path also takes us higher in the branches upon the Tree of Life, continuing our progression from *Malkuth* on to *Tav* and now into the Sephirot of *Yesod*, the upper most reaches of the physical world and the place upon the allegorical tree between which all realities pass. Thus, this mastery is the foundation upon which all future progression and growth is predicated.

As a degree, the Master step is the culmination of
the two before it and expressed as the potentiality
of our journey into the world — analogous to the
journey within which, like a *Mobius strip*, returns
its travelers to the exterior expression of the mind.
It is the Alpha and the Omega, the beginning
and the end. In its culmination, it is the transition
through life and death in order to be reborn anew
with an understanding of the spiritual world that
has always been around us but now made visible. Here, the moon is key, as *Yesod* leads to our
understanding of becoming an emblem of the
reflective nature we assume in this transformation.
Like the moon, we reflect the light of the Great
Architect, capturing what is impossible to see
without becoming blinded by its radiance. This
is, of course, a metaphor but no less appropriate
to the change we undergo and the purpose we
assume in becoming masters. Like the moon, each
of us reflects the glory of the divine sun in phases,
exerting our gravitational force over the tides
of our interactions. By undertaking this degree,
we become the *Anima Mundi* — the soul of the

world — created from the stuff of the earth and born of stars, existing between the firmament and the heavens. This is the greatness of our transformation!

THE GREAT WORK

We have up until this point sought Light and, like the moon, are now reflective of it. Yet, the moon as this symbol gazes directly into the source of its radiance and is what we seek ultimately to achieve. Emerging from our sanctum as masters, it is here that we put our practice into action and take our place at the top of our climb into the inner chamber. This journey requires only one additional step, but the one that is the hardest to take. We must undergo a sacrifice so severe that few willingly accept it, while those who do celebrate in the freedom it provides. Our guide in this step is represented in the figure of Grand Master Hiram Abiff, whose integrity and unwillingness to compromise his ethic are rewarded in the most horrible manner — which is a gift to us, as we need only study his fate to avoid suffering the same outcome.

The binding of our twofold tether is emblematic of the *Ouroboros,* which now coils a third time to bind the span of the eternal cosmos with that of the eternal soul — giving beauty to the strength of wisdom that comes from knowing the soul of the cosmos. This knowledge is our everlasting strength of fraternity, equality, and liberty, and our chain of union in spiritual enlightenment. With reverent gaze, look upon the vessels of corn, wine, oil, and salt to see them as earthly elements of transformation. The corn represents generation of multitude, each kernel of which grows and multiplies in each turning season. Wine, the elixir of Dionysus, is the product of a chemical transformation, an alchemy of combination and transubstantiation, which has as its capacity to bring joy and misery through its consumption. Oil is the spiritual anointment from the natural plant capable of cleaning all manner of sin and conducting as a lens focuses light. And salt — the essence of the earth, abundant in the seas and in the soil — is the essence of which in moderation enhances and preserves all it mingles with, yet when taken in mass can destroy and cause severe illness and death. These symbols, taken together, become a transformative alchemy with both cause and effect and the now mercurial transformation dearly sought by all seekers of wisdom.

The cycle of becoming a master is an attempt to awaken the spirit within in order to gain new perspective from it. Some traditions hold this initiation through a baptism of water. In others, it comes in a passage of age or achievement. In the *Hermetic* tradition, Hermes Trismegistus says it is the willingness to be "immersed into a mixing bowl," which is an allegory to being *immersed* into wisdom — the gift of mind representing the divine and our willingness to be *immersed* into it. As such, this degree is its parallel, and our willingness to be *immersed* into it is our willingness to be *immersed* into the cosmos and receive knowledge of things divine and shape those gifts into wisdom. This lesson is one Albert Pike, the great author of

Morals and Dogma, taught and gave to us in his essay on the second degree. "Knowledge," he says, "is convertible into power," but not itself power. "Wisdom," he says, "is power" whose governance comes out of justice, which is "the perfected law of Truth." He concludes this thought saying, "the true object of Masonry...is to add to your estate of wisdom and not merely your knowledge." This is the allegory of Freemasonry and your immersion into the divine knowledge which gives you wisdom.

Thus, this is the final passage of the symbolic lodge that awaits us. Our only impediment is our need to enter into the degree. As the moon moves through its phases, our moon is in full gaze of the Light which signals us to enter into our initiation. The *Sephirot of Yesod* is before us as our journey to mastery begins with the obligation of the Master Mason. We ascend the final steps to gaze through the window of the cosmos and merge our mind with that of the divine.

Clear your thoughts, offer a prayer to the deity (as no great undertaking should be made without first invoking God) and allow this invocation to the divine aspect you hold as truth guide your thoughts to the task at hand.

The Great Work awaits.

We Worship
Immutability!

ALBERT PIKE
MORALS & DOGMA
THE APPRENTICE DEGREE

———————————

Where were you
when I laid the foundation of the earth?
Tell me, if you have understanding.

JOB 38:4

ANIMA MUNDI
GREGORY B. STEWART, PEN AND INK
2017

THE
MASTER MASON

The Reason of Being

"To be or not to be" are the immortal words written by the eminent bard of Avon, William Shakespeare. His question appears in the story of Hamlet posed by a lost son striving to find answers to what would, by most, be an unfathomable question — which is the essence of the third degree. "To be" is perhaps the oldest of the *New Age* paradigms, stirring echoes across theologies of all cultures said best in the application of the *Golden Rule* — as to do unto others which is *Being* itself. Like the *Golden Rule*, in order to do unto others, we must first understand ourselves, the innerness of our being, such that we can *Be* in the first place.

This lesson is not something that is unique to

the fraternity of Freemasonry, or this degree, as
we find the idea of the *Golden Rule* transcribed
across millennia and within every theological
system.[1] So too do we find the testament as a personal gospel of finding *our* truth. For most, truth
is mythology whose philosophical lessons are lost
in the dogmas of its authority — its commen-
taries on the philosophies become more valuable
than the philosophies themselves, and the value
of what was said is lost to the dominion of those
who hold authority over them. We must interpret
the truths for ourselves to find their resonance
within us. This is the entirety of the lesson of the
third degree, the marrow in the bones of antiquity
within which the truth spans all landscapes — if
the seeker looks deeply enough into its composition. But, as with any concept, truth is itself
mutable as generations add or redact its communication, creating ever-fluctuating permutations
and confluences of its principle concepts. Truth
is truth, no matter how others dictate its interpretation. It is our own internal mechanisms that
decide it for ourselves.

THE REASON OF BEING

For the Mason reading, we, as Hiram, per-
ish in custody of our virtue, which in turn is the
vehicle of our metaphoric resurrection in being
made perpendicular again, a zenith we find in the
number three as the union between one and two,
duality itself made whole. By reading the degree,
whether in the Scottish or York Rite telling, the
overtones are distinctly Christian, but like the
Christian Church itself, the tradition existed well
before the consummation of the Gospels and
illustrate the depth of antiquity for what they seek
to convey. As with every symbolic story, we must
look at it through filters and adjudge the entirety
by the description of the pieces to achieve a level
of perspective over the totality within which it
exists.

Freemasonry is, if anything else, a conglom-
erate of ideas, culled together from a variety of
sources. So then, to understand its summation we
need to look at the Kabalistic connections of this
degree as it relates to our Tree of Life progression, (see *The Apprentice* and *Fellow of the Craft*)
as the degree of the Master Mason resides within

the *Sephirot of Yesod* on the pillar of mercy giving several meanings and parallels. So too will we do well in finding its corresponding relations in the Tarot as Yesod relates to the cards of the Four Nines, which is also a source of its symbolic origin. But, our greatest understanding will come as we look at the degree itself to understand why the master mason is arranged the way it is, given its discordant portrayal when compared with the two that preceded it in both presentation and tone.

No longer is the degree about simply the teaching of ideas and social principles, nor is it an indoctrination meant to introduce foreign concepts to the newcomer. No, this degree is about the inner journey, the making of the "transcendent transparent" which it does by introducing, in its present-day conduct, an aspect of itself that strives to teach its lesson through theatrics in order to convey its lesson in a manner reminiscent of a morality play with antecedents common at the time of its ritual organization. "To be...or not to be," that is the challenge that faces each of us as we confront our own inner Hiram and is the question which will open the door of the future of Masonry in the pursuit of the higher degrees. The esoteric writer Eliphas Lévi says in his book *The History of Magic*, "Ordeal is the great word of life, and life itself is a serpent which brings forth and devours unceasingly." Man is born into chaos to seek light from that which he was created which, the great tradition of *Hermetica* tells us, is but merely a reflection, as the moon reflects the light of the sun — an aspect of this tradition we find in the parallel with Yesod. Thus, we need a place to begin our study, and where best to begin than with the number of the degree itself so as to construct an understanding of the significance of the number three and its relationship to many other traditions as the unifying force of division.

As this is the pinnacle in the Symbolic Lodge system, the third degree is itself an underlying symbolic construct that predates its inclusion in the Masonic system. Cirlot, in his *Dictionary of Symbols*, says that in earlier times the use of the number three was "a symbol that has significance with the goddess of [the] woods, Diana, in her

Greek appellation of Hecate…she who succeeds from afar." The figure of Diana holds characteristics that "vary with the phases of the moon" and are represented by the images created by Diana, Jana, and Janus. In some representations, the goddess Hecate is depicted with three heads, which is a triune form, an "inversion of the Trinitarian form of the upper world" and symbolic in the underworld to the "perversion of the three essential 'urges' of man: conservation, reproduction, and spiritual evolution."[2]

But, Cirlot also looks at the number as the "spiritual synthesis" and the "formula for the creation of each of the worlds." It is, he says, representative of the "solution of conflict possessed by dualism" and expressed in the half circle, which is demarcated through the cycle of birth, manhood, and death as well as the points of the triangle.[3] This expression, he suggests, is concerned with "basic principles, and express sufficiency, of the growth of unity within itself," which is an aspect we can find in many traditions, perhaps most clearly in the Christian idea of the trinity. The

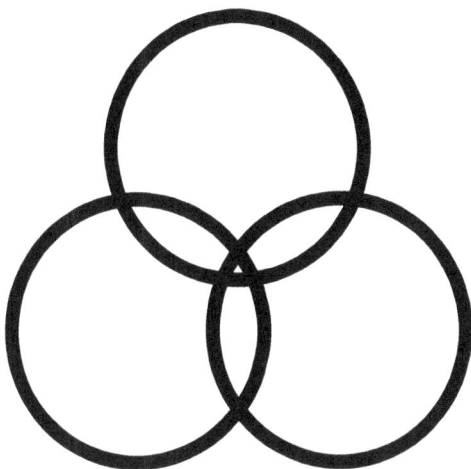

TREFOIL (WITH THREE FOLD LEAF)
KNOWLEDGE OF THE DIVINE ESSENCE GAINED BY HARD ENDEAVORS,
THROUGH SACRIFICE OR STUDY

trefoil is a reminder of this in its representation of "knowledge of the divine essence gained by hard endeavors, through sacrifice or study," which is the idea of ascension or spiritual elevation.[4]

Numerical significance cannot go unnoticed in many of the sacred traditions where the tryptic aspects of balanced unity can be found in Sumerian deity worship (Anu, Enlil, and Ea), Babylonian worship practice (Sin, Shamash and Ishtar), the Greek goddess Hecate in her three forms (Sky, Earth and the nether world), the three strides of Vishnu in Hinduism as well as the *Brahma, Shiva* and *Visnu.* In Buddhism, it is represented in the three heavenly powers of *Amida, Sheishi* and *Kwannon.* Greek and Etruscan pantheons, of antiquity, were ruled by *Zeus, Athena* and *Apollo* as well as the Zoroastrian balance of dualism between *Ahura Mazda, Ahriman* and *Zurvan*, the god of time. We find the same need for balance in the Teutonic beliefs of Nordic tradition with *Odin, Wili* and *Weh.* Islam holds true to this pattern of three in that in the Shiite tradition, which is composed of the all-encompassing God, Mo-

hammed as the messenger of God and Ali, who
is the friend of God. Also, the broader tradition
of Islam holds the "Quaranic division of Islam
(surrender), Iman (faith) and Ishan (to do good)."
This same division appears in Sufism, which has
divided the way of mortals into shari'a (divine
law), tariqa (mystical path) and haqiqa (reality) —
ultimately culminating in marifa, or a final mystical knowledge.[5] In Judaism, we find representative
harmony where one signifies unity, two disagree-
ments, and three for the harmony that the oppo-
sites produce, finding resonance in the first three
days of creation. And, in perhaps a more obvious
overt fashion, in the Christian tradition of the
father, son and holy ghost (spirit), which in totality form the summation of the trinitarian deity
himself.

This numeric consideration should give us
ample understanding for why it is symbolically
significant, and why it would be impossible to
consider the degree system as a spiritual system
of wisdom communication without it. In a sense,
the balance of three is a necessity without which

ADONAI

PITAGORE

אדני

EZECHIEL

TETRAMORPH IN HERMETIC TRIANGLE
FROM TRANSCENDENTAL MAGIC ITS DOCTRINE AND RITUAL
BY ELIPHAS LEVI
FIG VIII – THE PANTACLES OF EZEKIEL AND PYTHAGORAS:
THE FOUR-HEADED CHERUBIM OF EZEKIEL'S PROPHECY, EXPLAINED BY THE
DOUBLE TRIANGLE OF SOLOMON. BELOW IS THE WHEEL OF EZEKIEL, KEY OF ALL
PANTACLES, AND THE PANTACLE OF PYTHAGORAS. THE CHERUB OF EZEKIEL IS
HERE REPRESENTED AS IT IS DESCRIBED BY THE PROPHET. ITS FOUR HEADS ARE
THE TETRAD OF MERCAVAH; ITS SIX WINGS ARE THE SENARY OF BERESCHITH.
THE HUMAN FIGURE IN THE MIDDLE REPRESENTS REASON; THE EAGLE'S HEAD
IS FAITH ; THE BULL IS RESIGNATION AND TOIL; THE LION IS WARFARE AND
CONQUEST. THIS SYMBOL IS ANALOGOUS TO THAT OF THE EGYPTIAN SPHINX,
BUT IS MORE APPROPRIATE TO THE KABBALAH OF THE HEBREWS.

we would be confronted with only a duality like the checker pavement of earlier degrees, devoid of transition or transformation. This process of decision bears some significance in the philosophical tradition of *Hermetica* as in the process of its creation mythology, the duality of infinite light is only separated by an equally infinite darkness, which it says is like dark water, the separation of which comes in the eruption of fire between them out of the breath of the word of creation from the mind of God.[6]

Perhaps, in a more masonic sense, we can see its significance in the union of double trigons as found in the Hermetic triangle and its combination of the microcosm and macrocosm, better known as the union of the square and compass which, in the degree, are shown with the points resting above the square and our point of origin upon entering the lodge. Of this particular symbol, Albert Mackey, in his *Encyclopedia of Freemasonry*, says it represents the union of two principals, active and passive forces much the way the mosaic pavement represents the light and dark.

By encountering this degree, we have, in a basic sense, reached the pinnacle of our development and the apex (or zenith) of enlightenment. This is not to say that we have learned all that we need to know but, like Abraham in the Judeo/Christian tradition, we have been shown the promised land for what awaits us to yet still learn and experience. As a third-degree Master, we are at a lodge zenith and have only begun looking deeper to understand our symbolic foundation.

Using that metaphor of ascension, we can build on this progression by looking to the Kabalistic correspondence of this work. Given our progression as an apprentice through the *Sephirot of Malkuth* and across the path of *Tav* as a fellow craft, our logical destination here is *Yesod* upon the *Tree of Life*. Israel Regardie, in his exploration of the working in the Golden Dawn, says Yesod is "that subtle basis upon which the physical world is based," that it is "the astral plane, which in one sense being passive and reflecting the energies from above." He associates that reflectiveness with the moon as it "reflects the light from the sun."[7]

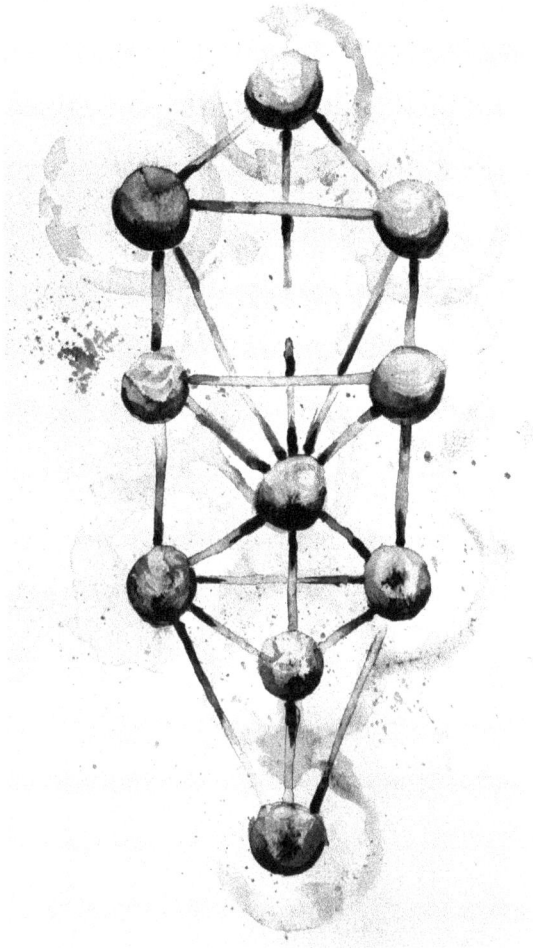

TREE OF LIFE
GREGORY B. STEWART, INK ON PAPER
2014

This gives us an interesting point to consider as each of us is said to be the child of the God, son or daughter, and said to be made in the divine's image. The text of *Hermetica* tells us that man was created as craftsman to create and govern with nature[8], which Regardie finds parallel as "Yesod is this stable foundation," a "changeless ebb and flow of astral [spiritual] forces, and the universal reproductive power in nature," where all "potentialities" exist and "go through this [Sephirot]." Here again we find in Regiardie's work a mention of the Roman Goddess Diana, who was symbolically depicted as the moon, which he says is the source of astral [spiritual] light and that the moon is said to produce it as it is the *"Anima Mundi"* or "soul of the world," which he likens to Carl Jung's "collective unconscious" as the psychological soul of the world.[9]

Athanasius Kirchner, the Renaissance theologian who wrote on the mysticism of Kabbalah, calls the Sephirot of *Yesod* the "collective intelligence," which he says "Astrologers, by the judgment of the stars and the heavenly signs, derive all speculation and the perfection of their science according to the motions of the stars."[10] Kirchner's astrological reference aside, he does give us an interesting aspect to consider, especially since the Sephirot is said to be representative of the moon, which, Cirlot says, is because of its pattern of change (itself a pattern of creation, destruction, and rebirth) that the moon has been seen in mythological tradition as the "mediator between earth and heaven [such] that lunar space [is] no more than one stage in the ascension which is the reason why the moon presides over the formation" of living things as well as their decomposition, ultimately the place within which "all realities pass." [11]

This is our zenith, at least in the attainment of this degree, and the moon is analogous to being, in the Hermetic view, of the reflection of the light of the sun, which is the mind of God, as we are the creator's craftsman who shape reality from his light.

So how is this illustrated in the presentation of the third degree? Before we explore the esoteric connection, we first need to understand the origin of the third-degree ritual and the environment from which it may have evolved. Understanding this will give us the context from which springs its antecedent of the fraternal drama we know today.

In his work *Masonic Orders of Fraternity*, Manly P. Hall suggests that the "rituals later associated with the degrees of Freemasonry may have been suggested by...guild dramas," which are more commonly referred to today as English mystery plays.[12] Hall writes, "Such theatrical performances were morality dramas rather than historical accounts and supplied a pattern for the ritualistic presentations now associated with the initiation rites of *Secret Societies*."

While Hall is perhaps over emphasizing the facts, it is accepted in scholarship that mystery plays have existed since the formation of the Christian Church and have, through the ages, evolved out of church liturgy incorporating very early aspects of what we would today consider acts in a play. Davidson, in his book *English*

FRONTISPIECE FROM A DISSERTATION ON THE PAGEANTS OR
DRAMATIC MYSTERIES ANCIENTLY PERFORMED AT COVENTRY
THOMAS SHARP, 1825

Mystery Plays, suggests that in the "liturgy of fourth century we see much more clearly the dramatic character of the service, which may be roughly divided into two acts...the first act is one of preparation; the second [leading] directly to the Eucharist, it's fitting climax."[13] This type of service practice in the third century was the result of centuries earlier when the Roman writer Pliny reported to Emperor Trajan that the first century Christians practiced a "divided service" where they met in the early morning for prayer and later for a communal meal.[14] As the Catholic Church manifested after Constantine, its rules and ritual expanded and so too did its conveyance of the mysteries adopting the style of Greek and Roman plays, similarly perhaps in the same manner they would "adopt the Roman Basilica as a church type, or plant Christmas upon the Roman holiday of Saturnalia."[15] These "dramas" evolved out of the church liturgy to become a part of their annual cycle in the liturgical year, in particular in the period of Christmas as a means to teach the liturgy of the birth of Christ through dramatizations which led to the *Corpus Christi Cycle* of plays (a dramatization suppressed in Protestant churches during the Reformation) to teach of the death and resurrection of Christ.

These plays remained in the church, to an extent, with varying degrees of practice from region to region with attributes unique to their place of performance; there they remained as a part of the service despite growing resistance from clergy over the play's secularization and popularization adopted by the societies they were performed by. Davidson says that "the plays did not leave the churches, but, in their less developed ritualistic form, remained a part of the service until the Reformation, and indeed in many countries...long after" and that "the plays were driven out of the churches by the disapproval of the higher clergy" because they "scandalized the devout and provoked the prohibitions and councils."[16]

In the period of the 15th century, guilds and fraternities flourished in Western Europe, but not in the manner we know of them today. Many of these guilds existed as religious societies com-

posed of ecclesiastics and lay members of churches, formed in part as religious "brotherhoods...
who were sometimes promoters of the religious
mystery plays." We can find an example of this
in the French Puy (or Pui Society), which was a
shadowy literary academy of the Middle Ages
who were "semi-religious, semi-literary" and
who "cultivated zealously the religious dramas."[17]
While this society began as a successor to the
clergy in the organization of the mystery plays in
France, in time they began to take on a "broader
literary life." Davidson suggests that as England
contained many French ecclesiastics in the later
eleventh and twelfth centuries, it would not be
surprising to find their influence in the church
guilds of England, especially when considered in
the abundance of religious plays organized and
performed by an equally abundant number of
guild halls with the purpose of presenting these
mysteries. By the beginning of the 1600s, the
mystery plays in England took on an aspect of
allegorical plays and presented as pageantry to
visiting royalty in whichever town they would

arrive in, and in some instances abandoned the plays because some guilds felt that the "pageants... were a heavy tax," considering their frequency and complexity.[18] It was in this late period that specific craft guild plays began to emerge and be presented in cycles relevant to the church. "In 1528 certain crafts acted plays during Christmas week before certain high officials," Davidson says, as that the plays they presented were chosen "in reference to the craft; thus the Taylors played Adam and Eve; the shoe makers, Crispin and Crispianus; the vintners, Bacchus and his story; the carpenters, Joseph and Mary; the smiths, Vulcan and what related to him; the bankers, a comedy of Ceres, the goddess of corn." In time, the craft guild plays evolved and were adopted into the theatrical presentations we find in the works of Shakespeare. Yet, as Davidson concludes, "the craft plays were the favorite literature of the people for about two centuries...in them are embedded phases of thought prevalent in successive generations of men."[19]

So how did these prevalent thoughts of successive generations of men become manifest in the fraternity of Freemasonry or free stone masons which congealed into the grand lodge system of 1717?

Tobias Churton, in his work *Freemasonry–the Reality*, explores this question and suggests the ascension of the craft blossomed with the ascension of Stuart James of Scotland in 1603, as the king was dubbed "the new Solomon" who had a "...penchant for poetry with a serious religious or moral theme" within which Masonic tradition, he says, holds that the king was an 'Admitted Mason' to Scottish Freemasonry."[20] That, in the growth of English power, "foreign trade" brought "money, merchants, and nobles" who were "desirous to spend to the magnificence of the new Solomon."[21] But Churton says that the stone mason guilds were not, perhaps, as prevalent as the Marblers guilds, as "most buildings were done in brick" while "the best structures were raised in stone," essentially decorative work done by workers in marble who "merged with the freemasons in 1585."[22] This observation shows us the pres-

ence of the masons guild but not their rituals, nor
is there any mention of the stone mason guilds as
presenters of styled mystery plays in the records
that remain, which may speak to their having
been a small guild of traveling workers rather
than a city-to-city established guild hall association. It is not until 1646 that we can find specific
mention of membership in the journal of Elias
Ashmole, who records that he was "…made a Free
Mason at Warrington in Lancashire."[23] Ashmole
does not record what, if any, play was presented to
suggest that he underwent some form of initiation that conveyed what we would regard today as
the modern ritual beyond the mere teaching of "a
secret word and grip" of initiation to the entered
apprentice and fellow craft degree.[24]

With this historical perspective in mind, it
may be prudent to suggest that the third-degree
ritual was an adoption from these guild liturgical
dramas, modified and applied to what was, at the
time, a two-degree system. The obvious question here is: Why add a third degree to a system
that likely existed and functioned long before its

master mason invention? Most likely, this inno-
vation rests in the advent of the Grand Lodge
of 1717 and a profession of restless fellow-crafts,
a limited amount of lodge masterships and the
need to inject a sense of progression into a system
of association fast becoming a speculative science
out of an operative one. The fraternity itself, existing long before 1717, likely included in a manner,
a third degree of some kind, and as such its symbolism was adopted and passed through iterations
becoming what we know today as the Hiramic
Legend and his 'raising' by the strong grip of
King Solomon. The same is true of the Scottish
Rite adaptation which follows the Webb-Preston
ritual but with some subtle adjustments to infuse
esoteric and symbolic overtones.

In the Scottish Rite ritual telling, the candidate of the third degree is admitted on the benefit
of the word of pass, which picks up the mystery
drama as the ritual questions how the candidate
is in possession of it. Immediately, it is questioned
if the fellow craft has been party to the "horrible
crime" for which the lodge is staged for.[25] The as-

sumption is that the candidate, having committed the murder, would be stained with Hiram's blood upon his hands and apron.

Found to be free of stains or blemish, the candidate is allowed admission "in the sacred name of God," which gives us a glimpse of the teachings to come in the higher degrees. Upon entering, the candidate is received upon two extended points of the compass, said to draw a parallel of the most vital organs of man — which rest within the chest along with the "…most important tenets of Freemasonry which are contained within the extended points [of the compass]…which are Friendship, Morality, and Brotherly Love." Here we can see, perhaps, a vestige to the mystery of the teaching in this allegorical play.

At this junction of the ritual, the candidate is shown "the solemn paraphernalia of death" in order to "contemplate the momentous mysteries attendant upon man's final lying down to rest in the arms of the dread conqueror" death.[26] It continues saying "of dust thou art — to dust thou returnith" but not "…of the soul." That, in this context, we should reflect not on death itself but be appalled "…when our dear friends are suddenly sent by the inhumanity of man to their final resting place, to stand unannounced…before the maker." Clearly this is in reference to the death of Hiram Abiff (or in a broader context violence itself), who was violently murdered and not allowed to meet a natural end at the hand of time.

Finding the fellow of the craft free of complicity in the death of Hiram, the master of the lodge turns the candidate to the East, presenting for his view a "sad object" of death — a small skull — whose meaning is said to say "I have been, and I am no more," and whose further allegorical teaching is to suggest "all of the evils which oppress mankind." It is here in the ritual that the Grand Master Hiram is announced as the possessor of the "necessary qualifications constituting perfection," where the ritual states that he also comes from the lands "from which we receive our light [knowledge/wisdom]," that he "labored diligently at the erection of that spiritual temple which is destined to unite us all in one common worship

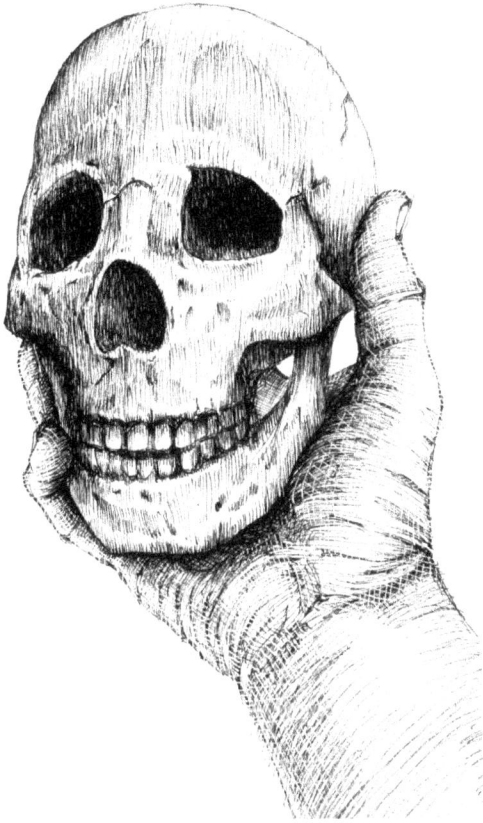

A Sad Object of Death
Gregory B. Stewart, Pen and ink
2017

— that of Truth."[27]

The country from which we receive our light is an interesting aside. In some Masonic traditions, it is speculated that Hiram comes from the tribe of Naphtali, whose origins comes out of the lineage of Jacob, which in *Genesis 46:24* speaks of the tribe's progenitor, who had moved to Egypt, setting their home and burial there, until such time his family [tribe] remained until the Exodus.[28] This could be construed to suggest, in the ritual, its connection to the religious or philosophical practice that predates Christianity and has aspects of the Egyptian mysteries or even the Hermetic aspects of monotheism and possibly Judaism, which are suggested to have emerged from such a lineage.

Here in the degree, the candidate is instructed that he will undertake three voyages said to represent youth, manhood and old age. Following the journey through the lodge room, the candidate is told "at the conclusion of mans tumultuous voyage of life, his every action passes in quick review before him, and the various scenes of his life

come to his mind with the …speed of thought,"
and that to die happily is "the man who can lay
to his final rest with a conscious void of offense
to God or man…with a forgiving and resplendent
heart." The ritual suggests a reading of *Ecclesiastes
12* during the voyage, which encapsulates the purpose of the "life well spent," with the concluding
admonition to fear God and keep his commandments, for this is the duty of all mankind, for God
will bring every deed into judgment, including
every hidden thing, whether good or evil.[29] This
gives us an interesting glimpse of the work in the
subsequent degree cycle, but more importantly, an
understanding of what it means to be a Mason
here and now, to essentially do good as the divine
sees all, no matter how hidden.

It is here that we encounter the higher symbolism of the degree, which follows the actual
making of the Master Mason by the candidates
taking of the obligation. In the Scottish Rite
working, following the obligation, the lecture sets
the stage for what will become the dramatic presentation of future degrees, which are steeped in

the liturgical mystery-play tradition of the church. In the opening of the lecture, the newly made Master is told the history of how Hiram Abiff came to be in the making of the temple. Hiram, King of Tyre, it says, brought the stone cutter and carpenter Adoniram to superintend the workman of wood and stone, and King Solomon brought Hiram Abiff to superintend the workman in Iron and Brass. Hiram Abiff, as this Masonic tradition tells us, "was filled with wisdom and understanding" so much so that he was made the chief amongst the workers and held as a 'brother' to King Solomon and King Hiram who, adopted "certain signs, words and grips," so as to enable "the various orders and classes to distinguish one from another." This (degree) was essentially the imagined creation, in dramatic form, of the system of builders — symbolic of the fraternity — from which is practiced today.

But here the degree lecture turns and adopts the style of the mystery play as the candidate is retired from the lodge room and returned to play the role of Hiram in a dramatic retelling of

what befalls the wise and understanding Grand
Master, who is so symbolic in this system. Unlike its Webb-Preston (blue lodge) counterpart,
this degree leaves the outcome of the degree to
a future telling and does not resolve the story as
the presentation concludes. But the narrative of
the degree telling proceeds to explain some of the
various symbolism at work to convey its themes.

Immediately, the mystery play begins with
Hiram's first confrontation with the fellow-craft
workman, Jubela, at the south gate of the temple.
Armed with a twenty-four-inch gage (or ruler), he
demands the grip of a Master Mason. Refusing,
Jubela strikes Hiram, sending him away, bloody,
to the west gate where he encounters fellow-craft
Jubelo, who confronts him with a carpenters (or
masons) square — demanding the grip which he,
too, is refused. Hiram, admonishing his attacker,
says he should "wait until the completion of the
temple" when, if found worthy, he would receive
it. Staggering and weak, Hiram stumbles his way
to the east gate, only to be confronted by the third
villain, Jubelm. Wielding a large hammer styled

as a setting maul, Jubelm demands again the word and grip of a Master Mason and is refused on the grounds that he has not earned it and by giving it would violate Hiram's honor and integrity. Hearing this, the enraged ruffian delivers a killing blow upon Hiram.

This brings us to a point of confusion in the lodge room as the scene in the degree transitions to the audience chamber of King Solomon, who is approached by nine fellow-craft masons who have come to confess their complicity in the plot to take the word and grip from Hiram. Sensing their desire for atonement for their complicity, Solomon sends the fellow-craft to find Hiram's remains, which they accomplish and mark them with a sprig of acacia.[30, 31]

The third act opens with Solomon's arrival at the grave to recover the body of Hiram from "the dead level to the living perpendicular." In broader context, the symbolism is explained as "the great law of our physical being: that all have to pass through the gates of death in our journey to the higher life," which is itself a metaphor of sorts to a both in life and death.[32] Solomon continues, saying "Truth, Fidelity, and Justice, portrayed as the elements to God and love of man, made the chief cornerstone of that spiritual temple, not made with hands, eternal in the heavens," so that we "ever remember that man is the architect of his own life and that the life of a great man reminds us we can make our lives sublime, when departing leaving behind us footprints on the sands of time."[33]

This conclusion gives us some sense of the *Sephirot of Yesod* and Regardie's idea of the subtle reflection here of the Good above. From the text of *Hermetica*, we find the aspect of Good as only coming from the divine light, and our ability in this degree a mere reflection of that divine light.[34] Integrity is what held Hiram to the end, his wisdom and understanding made manifest to hold the three fellows-of-the craft to their obligation — which, ultimately, resulted in the loss of his own life while preserving it. With Hiram in his grave, the three ruffians Jubela, Jubelo and Jubelm on the run, all that remains is the reflection of the honor of Hiram whom the candidate is composed as. But this is not the conclusion of this act as Solomon, attempting to raise Hiram with the apprentice and fellow-craft grips, descends into the grave proclaiming that he will "raise the body on the strong grip of the Lion's Paw, the lion of the Tribe of Judah," upon which the substitute for the (now lost) Masters word will be given "until the wisdom of future generations shall discover the True Word." With the hand of the Grand Master in his own, Solomon raises the body, instructing afterward that both Hiram and the candidate in the character were "raised from a dead level to a living perpendicular." Dramatically spectacular, this begs the question: Is this a literal resurrection, returning the deceased back to life, or a metaphor for something else?

While this entire conclusion is rife with symbolic overtones, the most compelling is the overt use of the Christian "Lion of the tribe of Judah" appellation which is found in *Genesis 49:9*[35] and again in *Revelation 5:5*[36], and in both instances used in reference to Judah, the son of Jacob and

the root of the line of David — a figure discussed
in the first degree as symbolic of the mystical
journey between heaven and earth.[37] Theological
discussions aside, here at the end of the degree we
are given this allegorical resurrection, not directly
by the Christ narrative (a prefigurate to the time
of Solomon), but by Judah, the son of Jacob, the
hand of integrity capable of opening the book of
seals in the Revelation, an aspect that the degree
itself likens as "emblematic of immortality," sym-
bolized by the crowing with a wreath of flowers
as antithetical to the resurrection or rebirth in the
afterlife — itself a symbol which dates to Greek
and Roman times.[38] In our representational role
as Hiram, we become, in effect, the third degree
itself — life, death and rebirth — as the completion of the symbolic lodge cycle.

But, what does Pike say in his analysis, and
how does he approach all of this symbolic theater
in his examination of the Master Mason Degree?
Early in his commentary in *Morals and Dogma*,
Pike points out the transition of the third degree
as a sacred drama "within which the Divinity is

revealed." Acknowledging the importance to both Pagan and Christian practice, Pike loosely gives us a connection to the liturgical mystery plays of only a few centuries earlier of Pike's writing in 1870. He says of these dramas that they "present its symbols to us, and add nothing by way of explanation," a "text without the commentary" which evades the "gloss that lead[s] to error and heresy and persecution." He goes on, saying, "these mystic shows and performances" were the "opening of a problem...calculated to arouse the dormant intellect."[39]

The lesson of the degree, Pike says, strives to teach the "divine in human nature," which "disappears, [as] interest, greed, and selfishness" takes its place. Here we can see an acknowledgement of Hiram's integrity which Pike interprets as encompassing the whole degree, saying that "justice to others and to ourselves is the same; that we cannot define our duties by mathematical lines ruled by the square, but must fill with them the great circle traced by the compasses; that the circle of humanity is the limit, and we are but the

point in its center..."[40] This is a lesson the aspirant
fellow of the craft learns upon his entry into the
lodge of master masons when he was met by the
points of the compass upon his breast. Pike says,
"A sentence is written against all that is unjust,
written by God in the nature of man and in the
nature of the Universe, because it is in the nature
of the Infinite God."[41] This nature of God and the
universe is the foundation of the *Sephirot of Yesod*,
that place in which all realities pass — the *Anima
Mundi* or Soul of the World. Our role as master is
to seek that divine nature.

It is in this path towards that divine nature
that these symbolic degrees, and this degree in
particular, that we find in Pike's writing his philosophical link to Hermes Trismegistus, the personification of whom we find in the writings of *Hermetica*. Pike, in *Morals and Dogma*, constructs the
genesis of the Egyptian *Horus* (from the land of
which Hiram is said to of come) and follows his
name's pronunciation as it transforms to Hiram
(or Hermes), the Kadmos, or the *Divine Light*
of wisdom saying, "KHURUM, therefore, im-

properly called Hiram, is KHUR-OM, the same as Her-ra, Her-mes, and Her-acles, the *'Heracles Tyrius Invictus,'* the personification of Light and the Son, the Mediator, Redeemer, and Savior." While this may be a fanciful genealogical examination, it does speak to an underlying subtext of thought, just as the mystery plays came at a time when the church overlaid its liturgical holidays on to pre-existing traditions. Is the literal lineage a dictate of meaning, or does it exist in the spirit of the idea at work behind the names we look to?

Yet, Pike supports the lesson at work in the degree, saying, "men may betray; principles never can" such that integrity is the "master's word." He adds, "Yield it up [the masters word] neither to flattery nor force! Let no defeat or persecution rob you of it."[42]

It is here in *Morals and Dogma* that Pike reveals to this system its lineage to the Kabbalah, as he suggests similarity to that of the Egyptian Triads which he breaks down as "the Father or spirit of action, an active principle of generative power, the Mother, or matter or the Passive Principle or the conceptive power and the son, Issue or Product, the universe, preceding from the two principles." He associates these terms with Osiris, Isis, and Horus, suggesting it is in "the same way, Plato gives us Thought the Father; Primitive Matter the Mother; and Kosmos the World, the Son, the Universe animated by a soul."[43] This construct is a parallel we can find in both the symbolic degrees, but also in the three pillars that compose the super structure upon which the Kabalistic Tree of Life is situated and where the first three degrees reside upon the middle pillar of Kosmos, the son of thought and matter. Further, Pike relates this idea to the construction of the perpendicular to represent "…the masculine nature, the base the feminine, and that the hypotenuse is to be looked upon as the offspring of both; and accordingly the first of them will aptly enough represent OSIRIS, or the prime cause; the second, ISIS, or the receptive capacity; the last, HORUS, or the common effect of the other two."[44]

Paul Foster Case, in his book *Esoteric Keys of Alchemy,* calls this Egyptian Triad the *First Matter*, which is a "perfect unity," meaning it has a perfectly homogeneous construct including aspects of this First Matter as being composed of sulfur, mercury, and salt. Case associates this composition with the four elements: fire, water, air, and earth. He says of them that they are "subtle or invisible entities...not to be understood to signify anything which is limited to the physical plane," and the principle of which he draws from the Hindu idea of *Tatva* (Tattwa) as the foundation of reality.[45] This *First Matter* also includes a fifth element which Case calls the "quintessence," from which the elements are derived from the principal of sound, or more specifically "the original power of vibration." Vibration, he says, can only be defined through the Hindu *Akasha*,[46] "the quality of...space...omnipresent...[which is] all pervading."[47] Case associates this summation with the "Apron worn by Freemasons," which is "a unity, representing the number three by its triangular flap, the number four by the square shape of the apron itself, and the number five by the five corners of the apron and flap combined."

Indeed the Pythagorean triangle to which Pike made association of greatest interest here is that the *First Matter* encapsulates all of the aspects of the three degrees which can be surmised in the totality of the configuration, the elements of plant, animal, mineral, man and adept (enlightenment) and for the four elements of fire, air, earth and water, which, when taken together, create the *First Matter* ruled by generation of Father, Mother, and Crone — the prime cause of Osiris — which is the receptive cause in Isis, and in the common effect in Horus. Taken abstractly, we can relate this to the degree which speaks of the practice that our ritual teaches as coming from Hiram's homeland, traceable to Egypt and the lineage of Naphtali.

Pike, it seems, sees this degree not as the apex of the teaching in totality but as the first step in the symbolic process. "Growth," he says, "is necessary for nations as for men. Its cessation is the beginning of decay." That, with "faith in man, hope for the future of humanity, loving-kindness for our fellows, Masonry and the Mason must

always work and teach." The course from the
degree continues to find that resonance with the
divine by *Being*. "The reason of Being, is Being
itself... Reason and science demonstrate to us
that the modes of Existence and Being balance
each other in equilibrium according to harmonious and hierarchic laws," that "this belief... is
in humanity, the most real of the phenomena of
being; and if it were false, nature would affirm
the absurd." Essentially, this becomes a secular
love of humanity, in essence Humanism, as love
of God because the being of God is humanity
itself, the *being of being*.[48] This is, at its most basic
thought, the essence of the Hermetic principle of
Mind in that the essence of God is the thought
of it being devoid of its creation, which is the
abstract of creation, the infinite light from which
creation emerges, an idea Pike echoes, suggesting
it as "The idea of God," which is to suggest that
"Humanity has never really had but one religion
and one worship.[49] This universal light has had
its uncertain mirages, its deceitful reflections, and
its shadows; but always, after the nights of Error,

we see it reappear, one and pure like the Sun" to which we, in this degree reflect that solar radiance in the Sephirot of Yesod reflecting the glory and light of the son/sun as the moon.[50]

Missing in this treatise is the exploration of its correspondence with the tarot. The reason for this is that it's association, while symbolic, is more so overt, rather than well woven into the fabric of its composition. To find its association, we must need look to the the groupings of cards of the nines, in particular here to the four nines as it is in them that we find the role of stability in change.[51] Under Aleister Crowley's *Thelema*, he says of the 4-nines that "although the Nines are cards of pleasure, it is the pleasure of illusion, since they are ruled by the faint light of Luna."[52] Here again we fall under the spell of the moon and it's animating light of the world. Change is the only conscious reality of world — whether overt or subtle, perceptible in the subtle movement of time, Yesod (the moon) remaining the constant always in a transitive state. Cirlot's *Dictionary* says of the number nine that "it is the complete image of the three worlds, and is the "end-limit of the numerical series before its return to unity."[53] How fitting to find change, so represented in an absolute fashion, seemingly not itself to be subject to its own necessity of change — it simply is, in all of its being.

It is here we reach the zenith of the degree in history, ritual and in analysis, yet left to ponder how it pertains to its place and arrangement in our world. We need to address this idea of *Being*, both in the deity and in ourselves which we can do by way of attempting to understand these symbols not as we are told to understand them in the Masonic context but in how we approach living them. Joseph Campbell, the scholar of mythology, says that a symbol is a "sign that points past itself to a ground of meaning and being that is one with the consciousness of the beholder," which is the truth within ourselves as we relate to the world creating, he says, quoting Karlfried Graf Durkheim, as "transparency to the transcendent."[54] In essence, this degree, as well as those before and after, gives us a mythological foundation by which we can weigh, measure and relate to our being in the world. To do this, Campbell suggests, we place "the emphasis on [our] own inward dynamic and then filtering out of the inheritance of traditions those aspects that support [us] in [our] own inward life," such that we are not tied to an inner life based on those traditions. This is the inner truth to which Pike alludes in his calling "nature" as the great teacher of man neither dogmatizing nor attempting to tyrannize by compelling to a particular creed or special interpretation. By doing so, we "employ nature's universal symbolism instead of the technicalities of language, [as it] rewards the humblest inquirer, and discloses its secret to everyone [in] proportion to his preparatory training and his power to comprehend them."[55] Or, as quoting Giordano Bruno, "God as absolute, has nothing to do with us," to which our pursuit in this degree is to find the transparency of transcendence, to be our Being in perfect harmony with the internal idea and external aspect of deity, which is our perfect perpendicular.[56,57]

At last, we can answer the question posed at the start of this exploration: are we "to be, or not to be?" In undertaking this degree we are without a doubt to *BE*, which is the answer. Though, this Being is not without its curiosities, and to exist in this Being, we must first be able to identify what that means and how to reach that understanding. As many traditions hold keys to achieve this perpendicular, within the Masonic tradition we have this degree which gives us the keys to open the door to other esoteric traditions, which include the *Sephirot of Yesod* and the even more abstract creations of the *Egyptian Triads* — which both Pike and Case make elaboration illustration of to illuminate the idea of completeness in the entire assemblage of the symbolic lodge. Truly, this degree opens as a mystery, especially as it is a vestige of the liturgical mystery plays whose origins can be traced to the earliest Church celebration in both content and context. This third degree give us three acts of drama which climax in a millennia old debate of life eternal as the *Prima Materia* — or First Matter. Yet, in reading into Pike's analysis, we can see his associations to the great philosopher Hermes Trismegistus who we find in the Hermetic texts. Given the first two degrees can only be linked to Ashmole's initiation, we can only hope to find parallels in other systems that share similarity to what that earliest biographer recorded in his diary. Perhaps by distilling down the degree to its most basic components, the trefoil is most representative of it in totality while the point within the circle encapsulated into the square is the strongest representation of the symbolic lodge as a whole, to which this degree culminates. This finds resonance with the four nines in the tarot as the shape of our desire through sheer will. Coming to this conclusion necessitates an examination of the symbolic degree system, which opens the door to the Lodge of Perfection. For now, we can be resolved to have achieved the zenith of our initiation into the Symbolic Lodge — seeking for wisdom, but finding integrity — as Truth, Fidelity and Justice give us the foundation upon which to become a Masters of the Craft.

LIVING AS A
MASON

"...there is no darkness
but ignorance...

WILLIAM SHAKESPEARE
TWELFTH NIGHT - ACT 4, SCENE 2, PAGE 3

In the Hermetic tradition, death is not a state
of being in so much as it is a state of transition,
the flux between energy and mass are separated
but not destroyed — as no "thing" in the universe
can be so. The shell of the human form is merely
deconstructed and returned to earth from whence
it came — a collection of carbon, minerals and
water. The spirit (or soul) is returned to the cosmic unfolding, which is the greater collected
unconscious of the deity that exists all around
us. Our very existence is the manifestation of the
being we so eloquently call God, which is the
greater idea of everything and the good we seek
in our existence. *Hermetica* teaches us that the ancients saw god as the only manifestation of *Good*

of which, like the moon reflecting the light of the sun, so too were we the physical reflection of the illumination from which we were formed. In the Masonic tradition, the legend of Hiram reminds us of that manifestation of good, the noble virtue of authority and derivative of the faithful endeavor. In Hiram's death, we find that a resurrection of the spirit comes from the Master's word. This parallel exists in most forms of Western faith taught at many levels and in many constructs. The Christ, by example, in his absolution of faith, and in its Judaic predecessor of prophecy that spoke of the once and future king, are two examples of transformation that its mythological hero undergo. But, for now, our existence in both heaven and hell exists for us here on earth, which is the creation of our own hands and the results of our own labor. Perhaps we can find more allegorical semblance in the three ruffians of how not to act out of accordance with the just and right. In both instances, death is our ultimate lesson, our leaving of the shell and the return to its radiance.

In part, this lesson is the one we learn in life —

LIVING AS A MASON

to do good, help one another and keep true to our faith from which we find the revelation of living and life. To accept life is to live and create, in emulation of the same craftsmen of the Hermetic source — both to build our inner spiritual temple and the manifestation of the temple here on earth so as to teach and show others the path, no matter what that sacred structure contains. Our work is about the construction of faith for those who come after us.

Living as a Mason

In a literal sense, you have already started living as a Mason when you chose to undertake the degrees and understand the symbolic lodge. In a metaphoric sense, you have progressed over time, like the lesson in the second degree, stepping from youth to middle age and now into maturity — placing yourself in a state of development between maturity and old age. As past degrees allude, the third degree brings us to a level of development which places us at the threshold of maturity and the allegorical death we must undergo so as to become our fullest potential in our next stage of being. Our ultimate transformation only occurs when our natural cycle reaches its completion and Fate, another Hermetic intercessory, dictates our time of metamorphosis.

In truth, there are four cardinal principles of Masonry which are supported by three tenets of its conduct. Using these as moral waypoints, they guide our existence as Masons and our future development within this philosophical movement.

The four cardinal virtues, as we have learned, are: *Temperance, Fortitude, Prudence* and *Justice.* Temperance instructs us to keep in moderation all that we do. Fortitude teaches us to find strength to weather adversity and build our resolve to what is right. Prudence alludes to wise decisionmaking and keeping rash behavior at bay, to govern one's self with discipline and reason. And Justice counsels us to see beyond the clouds of passion and prejudice to do what is right, just and fair in all dealings.

While these aspects are taught in an earlier degree, we must now embody them by example

and inculcate them into our life and actions —
which make us true Masons. Guiding these moral
ideals are the three tenants of Masonry: Brotherly
Love, Relief and Truth. Brotherly Love towards
all mankind, in particular to brothers and sisters
of the order; Relief of the distressed and those
unduly burdened in-so-far as your powers allow
you to do so; and Truth, which as we have learned,
is relative to each of us and provides a guiding
light illuminated by the wisdom of the *Golden
Rule* — which is the underlying principal of all
mankind, most especially ours, giving out proxim-
ity to its teachings.

When taken together, we then live the *Masonic
Life* and are recipients to the secrets of Masonry
and are now just and upright world citizens and
the champions of civil society.

This is what is at the heart of *Being* a Mason
means. Depending on our individual station or
place in life, and within the circles it operates,
our charge is to LIVE Freemasonry, which is to
be exemplary citizens as best able to support the
public discourse for the betterment of mankind.

This is the work in the quarry, led by the exemplar in Hiram, as a well-trained and experienced master craftsmen who serves as intermediary with kings, guiding the workman in the quarry to construct that temple to the divine.

Becoming a Master

The legend of Hiram, as you have read, is the story of a man who embodies that message of doing unto others and working for the betterment of society. His workman rewarded with the Masters Word at the completion of the temple allowed them to take it out into the world to continue their work. As such, our symbolic champion, Hiram, becomes the unwitting lesson of the perils that we meet in the world after facing great adversity and death.

Death then, in particular the death of Hiram, is not just a cessation of biological function. Rather, death is a redistribution of his wisdom to every craftsman created in his memory. In the Masonic tradition, death and return to life is an expression of all faith traditions — resurrection in Christianity; tradition of existence in Judaism; and the end of man's struggle and endeavor in Islam; through the transmission of spiritual energy into new Masons through his reincarnation in each of us assumed in the role of the three degrees. You are Hiram from the very beginning and, by your undertaking of this degree, are said to undergo his same transformation from life to oblivion. Your spirit within the fraternity is spread to all those who come after you. This gives us a sense of a funeral of sorts — for Hiram, for ourselves, for mankind — who lost its superintendent without understanding that his return to the cosmos is what has given us our commission to bring his light into the world, as we continue to build and construct in his image. Pikc links Hiram to Hcr mes and, in his writings on the third degree, to Horus, or perhaps even the more removed Sol, the solar sun in the heavens and the source from which all light emanates. It is that light from which we strive to reflect back into the world.

Whether allegorical or real, our death is not the end, but only the beginning of our existence as the labor and works we leave behind are the testaments of our love to those who come after us.

We find parallels in this as we consider the degree in relation to the Kabbalah and its correspondence to the *Sephirot of Yesod*, known as the *foundation of the subtle* upon which the physical world is based. Yesod, the closest metaphorical point to the sun, is the reflective illumination that casts its astral light onto the surface of the earth. This is the culmination of the degree in our journey inward to capture the illumination of the divine. This is the light we find at the apex of Jacob's ladder and in the fulfillment of our internal work upon the three, five and seven steps. Yesod is our point of transition from the Symbolic Lodge to the Lodge of Perfection — a point of transition emblematic in our becoming a Master.

So Mote it Be

ANIMA MUNDI
GREGORY B. STEWART, PEN AND INK
2017

FRONTISPIECE

Anima Mundi

The frontispiece is this work is an amalgam of sorts to the various traditions at work in a hermetic understanding of Freemasonry. In its summation, the board brings in elements of the first and second degree by means of the elementary armillary sphere at the bottom leading to the multi-storied tower (or ziggurat structure) crowned by the full moon. These elements, as described in the earlier works of this series, bring us, the viewer, in through a visual representation of the first two steps of the tree of life: First through the *Sepheriot of Malkuth*, the foundation; then up upon the path of *Tav* — our pathway from the firmament into the heavens. Here we approach the final leg of the journey to the symbolic lodge, becoming a master and gazing out into the universe for what — we believe — comes next.

Yet, still in firm grasp of this mortal coil, our understanding is only capable of taking in the visual length and breadth of the universe that we can actively perceive. To show us this universe is the reflective nature of our guide, the visage of the goddess Hecate embodied in the wild huntress of Diana and her bow, and ever-moving through the heavens only to present in her position of one brief instance before she hides herself again in quest of her divine lover, whose light she reflects. Yesod, the second Sepheriot, is the embodiment of the moon and reminds us of the Hermetic notion that just as God is the only thing good and true, we strive in our existence to achieve that goodness — only to ever capture it in reflection of its service.

Different than traditional tracing boards, this work is meant to capture the journey of the initiate — over the threshold from chaos through initiation, from the outer apartments up the 15 allegorical steps, to enter the *sanctum sanctorum* and the Holy of Holies for the sacred vision they encounter within through the transformation into a master with the Tree of Life (and now death) shrouded in the natural world while adrift in the cosmos. This sounds as the though it is a desolate and depressing void; rather, it marks the view within that comes through the allegorical death — metaphorical flash of light through the transitionary tunnel between waking and everlasting sleep. It is the cosmos, the reality we can see with the naked eye, illuminated by the light of wisdom — to show us time is vastly more over the threshold of the here and now before us. Is is not the darkness of night, nor the eclipse of the solar radiance. Instead it is the cosmic play at work night after night in the death and rebirth of Helios, a reminder that every rise of the solar disc is a new day replete with renewal and an opportunity to do again what was meant to be.

In its summation, this board is *Yesod*, the *Animus Mundi* — the soul of the world — that connects all living things and provides the foundation through its regular ebb and flow. Through it, all realities pass and with it the starting point of our self-awareness and the connection we share with the all.

This is the great awakening we achieve in becoming a master.

Acting Operatively as a Free Mason

As you have progressed and learned from the degrees thus far, the process of undergoing their teachings is, in a sense, a line of evolution. Not an evolution of the physical or an anthropomorphic change, but a subtler shift that takes place internally. It is an awakening of a primordial spirituality that serves to transcend the boundaries of our knowledge and the divine facilitating a conception of something broader. The lessons are almost remedial and discernable through any instructive medium or faith, but not necessarily with the context that comes with being initiated, passed and raised.

As we have learned, the underlying theme through the degrees of the symbolic lodge has been a progression of understanding — beginning with ones' own desire to undertake the degrees (as an apprentice) and then mature through them (as a fellow of the craft). Now, we find ourselves at the third degree — masters of the art.

Yet, unlike its predecessors, the lodge degree telling of this allegorical performance unfolds its teaching in a manner heretofore unseen, which transfigures the nature of the degree into something different and perhaps more beautiful. Rather than a strict monologue of instruction, we are thrust into a theatrical role assuming the place of our patron — Hiram Abiff.

In the drama, we experience several scenes that demonstrate his knowledge and virtue, while we are shown a subtext of desire, greed and murder in the three ruffians. When taken together with the role of Hiram, they serve as lessons in their own right. But now, we want to examine this degree as represented in a tracing board based on its design. While there are other boards from this tradition, most focus on the aspect of death which, as you have read, concludes the traditional degree architecture.

THIRD DEGREE MODERN MASONIC TRACING BOARD
GREGORY B. STEWART, DIGITAL COLLAGE
2008

Third Degree Tracing Board

Here in this tracing board, the focus of the teaching is on the transformation that the seeker undergoes in their quest towards becoming a master and member of the *virtuous fraternity*. Our journey upon the ladder and steps brings us to the gates of the temple, which ends in our allegorical death — the culmination of which being the faint glimmer of the divine spark as emitted from our creator. It is our choice to acknowledge this and complete our connection to it. And, like a faith tradition, the symbols and allegories are taught to create a common understanding with those who have traveled a similar path. The hope of completing this loop is the return to the Golden Rule, in that great proverb of *"do unto others as you would have done to yourself."* The allegory of the ruffians illustrates their own ignorance of this principle.

No one need maim and murder to comprehend this sentiment. Absolutely not! What we need to do is take the steps taught in all just and equitable societies to do better and lift up humanity to a place of prosperity. This is the lesson of all faiths indoctrinated in moral and dogmatic codes of man in their attempt to structure a system of social cooperation. But, as a Mason, we seek more than benign betterment, we seek to help others become craftsmen of the divine. By the effort we put into ourselves, so too do we channel that energy into external expressions of possibility for others.

It is in failing that lesson that the ruffians, flanking Hiram, represent the avarice and greed that manifest when vision fails and lust for power without the sacrifice of hard work takes hold. Through the loss of Hiram, the candidate in his stead preserves the stolen virtue in his sacrifice. In that death, the candidate experiences the violence that comes from greed.

Yet, that violence is not without its gift. On the board, we can trace the path from Hiram's passing, a metaphor for our own death, at the hands of the three ruffians and see that in this release we are able to transcend and make ourselves, in a fashion, like the Hermetic creators of the Great Architect — mankind made in God's image — with the power of both creation and destruction. Through these lenses of morality and personal growth, we become beacons of light, illuminating the path for others undergoing their own journey.

The attainment of the Master is the eternal representation of our choice of betterment. It is this transformative process at work in the board as, at its zenith, the transcended soul reaches towards the blazing star through the graces moving beyond the veil of heaven and the conception of the divine to that light of illumination, that state we all seek as the reward for the life well spent with its wisdom attained.

Through this process, we strengthen and build our fraternal bonds with mankind so as to no longer simply build temples to the divine but build the craftsmen that shape the temple stone. The work of the craftsmen is to craft understanding — of the life well spent, of the virtue of doing right and to teach and live the lesson of the Golden Rule. We find this principle in the many traditions of the *Great Work* and in particular our

Rosicrucian and Hermetic brothers and sisters in their earliest incarnations, which strove to observe and serve mankind through the administration of medical assistance and healing. This simple act, in an age of much sickness and distress, was a beacon of hope and future possibility in a world otherwise in eclipse from its barbarism, ignorance and domination by religious fervor. We, mankind, can help one another with need of moral reason or religious necessity. We help mankind out of love for our brethren and desire to alleviate their suffering. As this relief is not all together altruistic, as no such thing truly exists, we better our lot and share in this place as we treat others in a way we desire to be treated — for the betterment of all mankind.

Key Symbolism

This lesson is illustrated in the level of mankind, which implies we are all on an equal footing of life choosing our path and actions. The plumb is a reminder of our source above, whether it is a deity of cosmic spark, or a greater good. This is a lesson in something greater than ourselves and a point to which we can strive to attain greatness. The compass elevated above the square teaches us that this greater spiritual good supersedes the baser tenants and should circumscribe all of our decisionmaking. The 24-inch Gage is our means to measure our time, in the conduct of our day and throughout our life. This also is the lesson of the hourglass as our time on earth is measured and finite and need be used for the greater good. Lastly, the mallet and chisel are reminders of our hands and mind as they shape both the stones of our being and the blocks of society, which compose the structure of the world around us — without which, like having no moral conceptions the divine, we would be unable to shape the world around us with wisdom, strength, or beauty as these are lessons that come with time and practice of the royal art.

You may recall in the degree, Hiram admonishes the ruffians to pursue their work in order to earn the masters word. This lesson is a metaphor for the process of lifelong learning, which is itself the quest for that word and the understanding that comes from fulfillment of that quest. Each of us craves ownership of the lost word, but few put in the work to earn it.

These are the lessons of this tracing board and of this degree.

READINGS
ON THE
MASTER MASON

Didactics

Because of the nature of this work, it seems an appropriate inclusion to impart herein the ideas of other more notable expounders on the nature of what it means to be a Master Mason so as to establish the substance of the history behind its study. Many have applied pen to page on the meanings of Masonry and specifically on the Craft Degrees, some with a universal effect. These are just a few short excerpts from notable past Masonic authors. As you will note, much of this scholarship is nearly 100 years or more from the past. Be that as it may, the value of these words should weigh on the heart of any individual who has ascended to sanctum sanctorum.

Morals and Dogma
The Third or Master Mason Degree
by Albert Pike

To understand literally the symbols and allegories of Oriental books, as to ante-historical matters, is willfully to close our eyes against the Light. To translate the symbols into the trivial and commonplace is the blundering of mediocrity.

All religious expression is symbolism; since we can *describe* only what we *see*, and the true objects of religion are THE SEEN. The earliest instruments of education were symbols; and they and all other religious forms differed and still differ according to external circumstances and imagery, and according to differences of knowledge and mental cultivation. All language is symbolic, so far as it is applied to mental and spiritual phenomena and action. All *words* have, primarily, a *material* sense; however, they may afterward get, for the ignorant, a spiritual *non*-sense. "To retract," for example, is to *draw back*, and when applied to a *statement,* is symbolic, as much so as a picture of an arm drawn back, to express the same thing, would be. The very word *"spirit"* means *"breath,"* from the *Latin* verb *spiro, breathe.*

To present a visible symbol to the eye of another is not necessarily to inform him of the meaning which that symbol has to you. Hence the philosopher soon superadded to the symbols explanations addressed to the ear, susceptible of more precision, but less effective and impressive than the painted or sculptured forms which he endeavored to explain. Out of these explanations grew by degrees a variety of narrations, whose true object and meaning were gradually forgotten, or lost in contradictions and incongruities. And when these were abandoned, and Philosophy resorted to definitions and formulas, its language was but a more complicated symbolism, attempting in the dark to grapple with and picture ideas impossible to be expressed. For as with the visible symbol, so with the word: to utter it to you does not inform you of the *exact* meaning which it has to *me*; and thus, religion and philosophy became to a great extent disputes as to the meaning of words. The most abstract expression for DEITY,

which language can supply, is but a *sign* or *symbol*
for an object beyond our comprehension, and not
more truthful and adequate than the images of
OSIRIS and VISHNU, or their names, except as
being less sensuous and explicit. We avoid sensu-
ousness only by resorting to simple negation. We
come at last to define spirit by saying that it is not
matter. Spirit is — spirit...

The Mysteries were a Sacred Drama, exhib-
iting some legend significant of nature's changes,
of the visible Universe in which the Divinity is
revealed, and whose import was in many respects
as open to the Pagan as to the Christian. Nature
is the great Teacher of man; for it is the Revelation of God. It neither dogmatizes nor attempts
to tyrannize by compelling to a particular creed
or special interpretation. It presents its symbols to
us, and adds nothing by way of explanation. It is
the text without the commentary; and, as we well
know, it is chiefly the commentary and gloss that
lead to error and heresy and persecution. The earliest instructors of mankind not only adopted the
lessons of Nature, but as far as possible adhered

to her method of imparting them. In the Mysteries, beyond the current traditions or sacred and enigmatic recitals of the Temples, few explanations were given to the spectators, who were left, as in the school of nature, to make inferences for themselves. No other method could have suited every degree of cultivation and capacity. To employ nature's universal symbolism instead of the technicalities of language, rewards the humblest inquirer, and discloses its secrets to every one in proportion to his preparatory training and his power to comprehend them. If their philosophical meaning was above the comprehension of some, their moral and political meanings are within the reach of all.

These mystic shows and performances were not the reading of a lecture, but the opening of a problem. Requiring research, they were calculated to arouse the dormant intellect. They implied no hostility to Philosophy, because Philosophy is the great expounder of symbolism; although its ancient interpretations were often ill-founded and incorrect. The alteration from symbol to dogma is fatal to beauty of expression, and leads to intolerance and assumed infallibility...

Therefore no one need lose courage, nor believe that labor in the cause of Progress will be labor wasted. There is no waste in nature, either of Matter, Force, Act, or Thought. A Thought is as much the end of life as an Action; and a single Thought sometimes works greater results than a Revolution, even Revolutions themselves. Still there should not be divorce between Thought and Action. The true Thought is that in which life culminates. But all wise and true Thought produces Action. It is generative, like the light; and light and the deep shadow of the passing cloud are the gifts of the prophets of the race. Knowledge, laboriously acquired, and inducing habits of sound Thought — the reflective character — must necessarily be rare. The multitude of laborers cannot acquire it. Most men attain to a very low standard of it. It is incompatible with the ordinary and indispensable avocations of life. A whole world of error as well as of labor, go to make one reflective man...When men begin to reflect, they begin to differ. The great problem is to find guides who will not seek to be tyrants. This is needed even more in respect to the heart than the head. Now, every man earns his special share of the produce of human labor, by an incessant scramble, by trickery and deceit. Useful knowledge, honorably acquired, is too often used after a fashion not honest or reasonable, so that the studies of youth are far nobler than the practices of manhood. The labor of the farmer in his fields, the generous returns of the earth, the benignant and favoring skies, tend to make him earnest, provident, and grateful; the education of the market-place makes him querulous, crafty, envious, and an intolerable dullard.

Masonry seeks to be this beneficent, unambitious, disinterested guide; and it is the very condition of all great structures that the sound of the hammer and the clink of the trowel should be always heard in some part of the building. With faith in man, hope for the future of humanity, loving-kindness for our fellows, Masonry and the Mason must always work and teach. Let each do that for which he is best fitted. The teacher also is a workman. Praiseworthy as the active navigator is, who comes and goes and makes one clime partake of the treasures of the other, and one to share the treasures of all, he who keeps the beacon-light upon the hill is also at his post.

Masonry has already helped cast down some idols from their pedestals, and grind to impalpable dust some of the links of the chains that held men's souls in bondage. That there has been progress needs no other demonstration than that you may now reason with men, and urge upon them, without danger of the rack or stake, that no doctrines can be apprehended as truths if they contradict each other, or contradict other truths given us by God. Long before the Reformation, a monk, who had found his way to heresy without the help of Martin Luther, not venturing to breathe aloud into any living ear his anti-papal and treasonable doctrines, wrote them on parchment, and sealing up the perilous record, hid it in the massive walls of his monastery. There was no friend or brother to whom he could entrust his secret or pour forth his soul. It was some consolation to imagine that in a future age some one might find the parchment and the seed is found not to have been sown in vain. What if the truth should have to lie dormant as long before germinating as the wheat in the Egyptian mummy? Speak it, nevertheless, again and again, and let it take its chance!

Humanity has never really had but one religion and one worship. This universal light has had its uncertain mirages, its deceitful reflections, and its shadows; but always, after the nights of Error, we see it reappear, one and pure like the Sun.

The Secret Teachings of All Ages

The Hiramic Legend

by Manly P. Hall

The efforts made to discover the origin of the Hiramic legend show that, while the legend in its present form is comparatively modem, its underlying principles run back to remotest antiquity. It is generally admitted by modem Masonic scholars that the story of the martyred CHiram is based upon the Egyptian rites of Osiris, whose death and resurrection figuratively portrayed the *spiritual* death of man and his regeneration through initiation into the Mysteries. CHiram is also identified with Hermes through the inscription on the Emerald Table. From these associations, it is evident that CHiram is to be considered as a prototype of humanity; in fact he is Plato's *Idea* (archetype) of man. As Adam after the Fall symbolizes the Idea of human degeneration, so CHiram through his resurrection symbolizes the Idea of human regeneration.

Moreover, the Hiramic legend may be considered to embody the vicissitudes of philosophy itself. As institutions for the dissemination of ethical culture, the pagan Mysteries were the architects of civilization. Their power and dignity were personified in CHiram Abiff — the Master Builder — but they eventually fell a victim to the onslaughts of that recurrent trio of state, church, and mob. They were desecrated by the state, jealous of their wealth and power; by the early church, fearful of their wisdom; and by the rabble or soldiery incited by both state and church. As CHiram when *raised* from his grave whispers the Master Mason's Word which was lost through his untimely death, so according to the tenets of philosophy the reestablishment or resurrection of the ancient Mysteries will result in the rediscovery of that secret teaching without which civilization must continue in a state of spiritual confusion and uncertainty.

When the mob governs, man is ruled by ignorance; when the church governs, he is ruled by superstition; and when the state governs, he is ruled by fear. Before men can live together in harmony and understanding, ignorance must be transmuted into wisdom, superstition into an illumined faith, and fear into love. Despite statements to the contrary, Masonry is a religion seeking to unite God and man by elevating its initiates to that level of consciousness whereon they can behold with clarified vision the workings of the Great Architect of the Universe. From age to age the vision of a perfect civilization is preserved as the ideal for mankind. In the midst of that civilization shall stand a mighty university wherein both the sacred and secular sciences concerning the mysteries of life will be freely taught to all who will assume the philosophic life. Here creed and dogma will have no place; the superficial will be removed and only the essential be preserved. The world will be ruled by its most illumined minds, and each will occupy the position for which he is most admirably fitted.

The great university will be divided into grades, admission to which will be through preliminary tests or initiations. Here mankind will be instructed in the most sacred, the most secret, and the most enduring of all Mysteries — *Symbolism*. Here the initiate will be taught that every visible object, every abstract thought, every emotional reaction is but the symbol of an eternal principle. Here mankind will learn that CHiram (Truth) lies buried in every atom of Kosmos; that every form is a symbol and every symbol the tomb of an eternal verity. Through education — spiritual, mental, moral, and physical — man will learn to release living truths from their lifeless coverings.

The perfect government of the earth must be patterned eventually after that divine government by which the universe is ordered. In that day when perfect order is reestablished, with peace universal and good triumphant, men will no longer seek for happiness, for they shall find it welling up within themselves. Dead hopes, dead aspirations, dead virtues shall rise from their graves, and the Spirit of Beauty and Goodness repeatedly slain by ignorant men shall again be the Master of Work. Then shall sages sit upon the seats of the mighty and the gods walk with men.

The Lost Keys of Freemasonry

Chapter 2, The Candidate

by Manly Palmer Hall

Under allegories unnumbered, the mystic philosophers of the ages, have perpetuated this wonderful story, and among the Craft Masons it forms the mystic ritual of Hiram, the Master Builder, murdered in his temple by the very builders who should have served him as he labored to perfect the dwelling place of his God.

Matter is the tomb. It is the dead wall of substance not yet awakened into the pulsating energies of Spirit. It exists in many degrees and forms, not only in the chemical elements which form the solids of our universe but in finer and more subtle substances. These, though expressing through emotion and thought, are still beings of the world of form. These substances form the great cross of matter which opposes the growth of all things and by opposition makes all growth possible. It is the great cross of hydrogen, nitrogen, oxygen, and carbon upon which even the life germ in protoplasm is crucified and suspended in agony. These substances are incapable of giving it adequate expression. The Spirit within cries out for freedom: freedom to be, to express, to manifest its true place in the Great Plan of cosmic unfoldment.

It is this great yearning within the heart of man which sends him slowly onward toward the gate of the Temple; it is this inner urge for greater understanding and greater light which brought into being through the law of necessity the great cosmic Masonic Lodge dedicated to those seeking union with the Powers of Light that their prison walls might be removed. This shell cannot be discarded: it must be raised into union with the Life; each dead, crystallized atom in the human body must be set vibrating and spinning to a higher rate of consciousness. Through purification, through knowledge, and through service to his fellow man the candidate sequentially unfolds these mystic properties, building better and more perfect bodies through which his higher life secures even greater manifestation. The expression of man through constructive thought, emotion, and action liberates the higher nature from bodies which in their crystallized states are incapable of giving him his natural opportunities.

In Freemasonry, this crystallized substance of matter is called the grave and represents the Holy Sepulcher. This is the grave within which the lost Builder lies and with Him are the plans of the Temple and the Master's Word, and it is this builder, our Grand Master, whom we must seek and raise from the dead. This noble Son of Light cries out to us in every expression of matter. Every stick and stone marks His resting place, and the sprig of acacia promises that through the long winter of spiritual darkness when the sun does not shine for man, this Light still awaits the day of liberation when each one of us shall raise Him by the grip of the Grand Master, the true grip of a Master Mason. We cannot hear this Voice that calls eternally, but we feel its inner urge. A great unknown something pulls at our heartstrings. As the ages roll by, the deep desire to be greater, to live better, and to think God's thoughts, builds within ourselves the qualifications of a candidate who, when asked why he takes the path, would truly answer if he knew mentally the things he feels: "I hear a voice that cries out to me from flora and fauna, from the stones, from the clouds, from the very heaven itself. Each fiery atom spinning and twisting in Cosmos cries out to me with the voice of my Master. I can hear Hiram Abiff, my Grand Master, crying out in his agony, the agony of life hidden within the darkness of its prison walls, seeking for the expression which I have denied it, laboring, to bring closer the day of its liberation, and I have learned to know that I am responsible for those walls. My daily actions are the things which as ruffians and traitors are murdering my God."

There are many legends of the Holy Sepulcher which for so many centuries had been in the hands of the infidel and which the Christian worlds sought to retake in the days of the Crusades. Few Masons realize that this Holy Sepulcher, or tomb, is in reality negation and crystallization — matter that has sealed within itself the Spirit of Life which must remain in darkness until the growth of each individual being gives it walls of glowing gold and changes its stones into windows. As we develop better and better vehicles of expression, these walls slowly expand until at last Spirit rises triumphant from its tomb and, blessing the very walls that confined it, raises them to union with itself.

We may first consider the murderers of Hiram. These three ruffians, who, when the Builder seeks to leave his temple, strike him with the tools of his own Craft until finally they slay him and bring the temple down in destruction upon their own heads, symbolize the three expressions of our own lower natures which are in truth the murderers of the good within ourselves. These three may be called thought, desire, and action. When purified and transmuted they are three glorious avenues through which may manifest the great life power of the three kings, the glowing builders of the Cosmic Lodge manifesting in this world as spiritual thought, constructive emotion, and useful daily labor in the various places and positions where we find ourselves while carrying on the Master's work. These three form the Flaming Triangle which glorifies every living Mason, but when crystallized and perverted they form a triangular prison through which the light cannot shine and the Life is forced to languish in the dim darkness of despair, until man himself through his higher understanding liberates the energies and powers which are indeed the builders and glorifiers of his Father's House.

Now let us consider how these three fiery kings of the dawn became, through perversion of their manifestation by man, the ruffians who murdered Hiram - the energizing powers of cosmos which course through the blood of every living being, seeking to beautify and perfect the temple they would build according to the plan laid down on the tracing board by the Master Architect of the universe. First in the mind is one of the three kings, or rather we shall say a channel through which he manifests; for King Solomon is the power of mind which, perverted, becomes a destroyer who tears down with the very powers which nourish and build. The right application of thought, when seeking the answer to the cosmic problem of destiny, liberates man's spirit which soars above the concrete through that wonderful power of mind, with its dreams and its ideals.

When man's thoughts rise upon the wings of aspiration, when he pushes back the darkness with the strength of reason and logic, then indeed the builder is liberated from his dungeon and the light pours in, bathing him with life and power. This light enables us to seek more clearly the mystery of creation and to find with greater certainty our place in the Great Plan, for as man unfolds his bodies he gains talents with which he can explore the mysteries of Nature and search for the hidden workings of the Divine. Through these powers the Builder is liberated and his consciousness goes forth conquering and to conquer. These higher ideals, these spiritual concepts, these altruistic, philanthropic, educative applications of thought power glorify the Builder; for they give the power of expression and those who can express themselves are free. When man can mold his thoughts, his emotions, and his actions into faithful expressions of his highest ideals then liberty is his, *for ignorance is the darkness of Chaos and knowledge is the light of Cosmos.*

In spite of the fact that many of us live apparently to gratify the desires of the body and as servants of the lower nature, still there is within each of us a power which may remain latent for a great length of time. This power lives eternities perhaps, and yet at some time during our growth there comes a great yearning for freedom, when, having discovered that the pleasures of sense gratification are eternally elusive and unsatisfying, we make an examination of ourselves and begin to realize that there are greater reasons for our being. It is sometimes reason, sometimes suffering, sometimes a great desire to be helpful, that brings out the first latent powers which show that one long wandering in the darkness is about to take the path that leads to Light. Having lived life in all its experiences, he has learned to realize that all the manifestations of being, all the various experiences through which he passes, are steps leading in one direction; that, consciously or unconsciously, all souls are being led to the portico of the temple where for the first time they see and realize the glory of Divinity. It is then that they understand the age-old allegory of the martyred Builder and feel his power within themselves crying out from the prison of materiality. Nothing else seems worthwhile; and, regardless of cost, suffering, or the taunts of the world, the candidate slowly ascends the steps that lead to the temple eternal. The reason that governs Cosmos he does not know, the laws which mold his being he does not realize, but he does know that somewhere behind the veil of human ignorance there is an eternal light toward which step by step he must labor. With his eyes fixed on the heavens above and his hands clasped in prayer he passes slowly as a candidate up the steps. In fear and trembling, yet with a divine realization of good, he raps on the door and awaits in silence the answer from within.

Chapter 5, The Master Mason

On the upper steps of spiritual unfoldment stands the Master Mason, who spiritually represents the graduate from the school of esoteric learning. In the ancient symbols, he is represented as an old man leaning upon a staff, his long white beard upon his chest, and his deep, piercing eyes sheltered by the brows of a philosopher. He is in truth old, not in years, but in wisdom and understanding, which are the only true measurement of age. Through years and lives of labor he has found the staff of life and truth upon which he leans. He no longer depends upon the words of others but upon the still voice that speaks from the heart of his own being. There is no more glorious position that a man may hold than that of a Master Builder, who has risen by labor through the degrees of human consciousness. Time is the differentiation of eternity devised by man to measure the passage of human events. On the spiritual planes of Nature, it is the space or distance between the stages of spiritual growth and hence is not measurable by material means. Many a child comes into this world a Grand Master of the Masonic School, while many a revered and honored brother passes silently to rest without having gained admittance to its gate. The Master Mason is one whose life is full, pressed down and brimming over with the experience he has gained in his slow pilgrimage up the winding stairs.

The Master Mason embodies the power of the human mind, that connecting link which binds heaven and earth together in an endless chain. His spiritual light is greater because he has evolved a higher vehicle for its expression. Above even constructive action and emotion soars the power of thought which swiftly flies on wings to the source of Light. The mind is the highest form of his human expression and he passes into the great darkness of the inner room illuminated only by the fruits of reason. The glorious privileges of a Master Mason are in keeping with his greater knowledge and wisdom. From the student he has blossomed forth as the teacher; from the kingdom of those who follow he has joined that little group who must always lead the way. For him the Heavens have opened and the Great Light has bathed him in its radiance. The Prodigal Son, so long a wanderer in the regions of darkness, has returned again to his Father's house. The voice speaks from the Heavens, its power thrilling the Master until his own being seems filled with its divinity, saying, "This is my beloved Son, in whom I am well pleased." The ancients taught that the sun was not a source of light, life, or power, but a medium through which life and light were reflected into physical substance. The Master Mason is in truth a sun, a great reflector of light, who radiates through his organism, purified by ages of preparation, the glorious power which is the light of the

Lodge. He, in truth, has become the spokesman of the Most High. He stands between the glowing fire light and the world. Through him passes Hydra, the great snake, and from its month there pours to man the light of God. His symbol is the rising sun, for in him the globe of day has indeed risen in all its splendor from the darkness of the night, illuminating the immortal East with the first promise of approaching day.

With a sigh the Master lays aside his tools. For him the temple is nearing completion, the last stones are being placed, and he slakes his lime with a vague regret as he sees dome and minaret rise through the power of his handiwork. The true Master does not long for rest, and as he sees the days of his labor close, sadness weighs upon his heart. Slowly the brothers of his Craft leave him, each going his respective way; and, climbing step by step, the Master stands alone on the pinnacle of the temple. One stone must yet be placed, but this he cannot find. Somewhere it lies concealed. In prayer he kneels, asking the powers that be to aid him in his search. The light of the sun shines upon him and bathes him in a splendor celestial. Suddenly a voice speaks from the Heavens, saying, "The temple is finished and in my faithful Master is found the missing stone."

Both points of the compasses are now lifted from under the square. The divine is liberated from its cube; heart and mind alike are liberated from the symbol of mortality, and as emotion and thought they unite for the glorification of the greatest and the highest. Then the Sun and Moon are united and the Hermetic Degree is consummated.

The Master Mason is afforded opportunities far beyond the reach of ordinary man, but he must not fail to realize that with every opportunity comes a cosmic responsibility. It is worse by far to know and not to do than never to have known at all. He realizes that the choice of avoiding responsibility is no longer his and that for him all problems must be met and solved. The only joy in the heart of the Master is the joy of seeing the fruits of his handiwork. It can be truly said of the Master that through suffering he has learned to be glad, through weeping he has learned to smile, and through dying he has learned to live. The purification and probationship of his previous degrees have so spiritualized his being that he is in truth a glorious example of God's Plan for His children. The greatest sermon he can preach, the greatest lesson he can teach, is that of standing forth a living proof of the Eternal Plan. The Master Mason is not ordained: he is the natural product of cause and effect, and none but those who live the cause can produce the effect. The Master Mason, if he be truly a Master, is in communication with the unseen powers that move the destinies of life. As the Eldest Brother of the lodge, he is the spokesman for the spiritual hierarchies of his Craft. He no longer follows the direction of others, but on his own tracing board he lays out the plans which his brothers are to follow. He realizes this, and so lives that every line and plan which he gives out is inspired by the divine within himself. His glorious opportunity to be a factor in the growth of others comes before all else. At the seat of mercy, he kneels, a faithful servant of the

Highest within himself and worthy to be given control over the lives of others by having first controlled himself.

Much is said concerning the loss of the Master's Word and how the seekers go out to find it but bring back only substitutes. The true Master knows that those who go out can never find the secret trust. He alone can find it who goes within. The true Master Builder has never lost the Word but has cherished it in the spiritual locket of his own being. From those who have the eyes to see, nothing is concealed; to those who have the right to know, all things are open books. The true Word of the three Grand Masters has never been concealed from those who have the right to know it nor has it ever been revealed to those who have not prepared a worthy shrine to contain it. The Master knows, for he is a Temple Builder. Within the setting of his own bodies, the Philosopher's Stone is placed; for in truth it is the heart of the Phoenix, that strange bird which rises with renewed youth from the ashes of its burned body. When the Master's heart is as pure and white as the diamond that he wears, he will then become a living stone — the crown jewel in the diadem of his Craft.

The Word is found when the Master himself is ordained by the living hand of God, cleansed by living water, baptized by living fire, a Priest-King after the Order of Melchizedek, who is above the law.

The Great Work of the Master Mason can be called the *art of balance*. To him is given the work of balancing the triangle that it may blaze forth with the glory of the Divine Degree. The triple energies of thought, desire, and action must be united in a harmonious blending of expression. He holds in his hands the triple keys; he wears the triple crown of the ancient Magus, for he is in truth the King of heaven, earth, and hell. Salt, sulphur, and mercury are the elements of his work and with the philosophical mercury he seeks to blend all powers to the glorifying of one end.

Behind the degree of Master Mason, there is another not known to earth. Far above him stretch other steps concealed by the blue veil

which divides the seen from the unseen. The true
Brother knows this, therefore he works with an
end in view far above the concept of mortal mind.
He seeks to be worthy to pass behind that veil
and join that band who, dishonored and unsung,
carry the responsibilities of human growth. His
eyes are fixed forever on the Seven Stars which
shine down from somewhere above the upper
rung of the ladder. With hope, faith, and charity
he climbs the steps, and whispering the Master's Word to the Keeper of the Gates, passes on
behind the veil. It is then, and then only, that a
true Mason is born. Only behind this veil does
the mystic student come into his own. The things
which we see around us are but forms — promises
of a thing unnamed, symbols of a truth unknown.
It is in the spiritual temple built without the voice
of workmen or the sound of hammer that the true
initiation is given, and there, robed in the simple
lambskin of a purified body, the student becomes
a Master Mason, chosen out of the world to be
an active worker in the name of the Great Architect. It is there alone, unseen by mortal eyes, that

the Greater Degrees are given and there the soul radiating the light of Spirit becomes a living star in the blue canopy of the Masonic lodge.

Chapter 6, The Qualifications of a True Master

Every true Mason has come into the realization that there is but one Lodge - that is, the Universe - and but one Brotherhood, composed of everything that moves or exists in any of the planes of Nature. He realizes that the Temple of Solomon is really the Temple of the Solar Man — Sol-Om-On — the King of the Universe manifesting through his three primordial builders. He realizes that his vow of brotherhood and fraternity is universal, and that mineral, plant, animal, and man are all included in the true Masonic Craft. His duty as an elder brother to all the kingdoms of Nature beneath him is well understood by the true Craftsman, who would rather die than fail in this, his great obligation. He has dedicated his life upon the altar of his God and is willing and glad to serve the lesser through the powers he has gained from the greater. The mystic Mason, in building the eyes that see behind the apparent ritual, recognizes the oneness of life manifesting through the diversity of form.

The true disciple of ancient Masonry has given up forever the worship of personalities. With his greater insight, he realizes that all forms and their position in material affairs are of no importance to him compared to the life which is evolving within.

W. L. Wilmshurst

The Meaning of Masonry
Chapter III, Further Notes on Craft Symbolism
Third, or Master-Mason's Degree

As high priest of his own personal temple he must have his bodily nature and its varied desires under foot. He must have developed strength of will and character to "walk upon" this chequer-work and withstand its appeals. He must also be able to ascend the winding staircase of his inner nature, to educate and habituate his mentality to higher conscious states and so establish it there that he will be unaffected by seductive or affrighting perceptions that there may meet him. By the cultivation of this "strength" and the ability to "establish" himself upon the loftier conscious levels he co-ordinates the two pillars at the porch way of his inmost sanctuary — namely, the physical and psychical supports of his organism — and acquires the "stability" involved in regeneration and requisite to him before passing on to "that last and greatest trial" which awaits him. "In strength will I establish My house that it may stand firm." Man's perfected organism is what is meant by "My house." It was the same organism and the same stability that the Christian Master spoke of in saying "Upon this rock will I build my church and the gates of the underworld shall not prevail against it."

During all the discipline and labor involved in attaining this stability there has shone light on the path from the first moment that his Apprentice's vision was opened to larger truth; light from the science and philosophy of the Order itself which is proving his "porch way" to the ultimate sanctuary within; light from friendly helpers and instructors; above all, light from the sun in his own "heavens," streaming through the "dormer-window" of his illumined intelligence and slowly but surely guiding his feet into the way of peace.

But now the last and greatest trial of his fortitude and fidelity, one imposing upon him a still more serious obligation of endurance, awaits him in the total withdrawal of this kindly light. Hitherto, although guided by that light, he has progressed in virtue of his own natural powers and efforts. Now the time has come when those props have to be removed, when all reliance upon natural abilities, self-will and the normal rational understanding, must be surrendered and the aspirant must abandon himself utterly to the transformative action of his Vital and Immortal Principle alone, passively suffering it to complete the work in entire independence of his lesser faculties. He must "lose his life to save it"; he must surrender all that he has hitherto felt to be his life in order to find life of an altogether higher order.

Hence the Third Degree is that of mystical

death, of which bodily death is taken as figurative, just as bodily birth is taken in the First
Degree as figurative of entrance upon the path of
regeneration. In all the Mystery systems of the
past will be found this degree of mystical death
as an outstanding and essential feature prior to
the final stage of perfection or regeneration. As
an illustration one has only to refer to a sectional
diagram of the Great Pyramid of Egypt, which
was so constructed as to be not merely a temple
of initiation, but to record in permanent form the
principles upon which regeneration is attainable.
Its entrance passage extends for some distance
into the building as a narrow ascending channel
through which the postulant who desires to reach
the centre must creep in no small discomfort and
restrictedness. This was to emblematise the discipline and up-hill labor of self-purification requisite in the Apprentice Degree. At a certain point
this restricted passage opens out into a long and
lofty gallery, still upon a steeply rising gradient,
up which the postulant had to pass, but in a condition of ease and liberty. This was to symbolize

the condition of illumination and expanded intellectual liberty associated with the Fellow-craft Degree. It ended at a place where the candidate once more had to force his way on hands and knees through the smallest aperture of all, one that led to the central chamber in which stood and still stands the great sarcophagus in which he was placed and underwent the last supreme ordeal, and whence he was raised from the dead, initiated and perfected.

APPENDIX

The Golden Rule

"Lay not on any soul a load that you would not want to be laid upon you, and desire not for anyone the things you would not desire for yourself."

Baha'i Faith – Bahu'u'llah

"Treat not others in ways that you yourself would find hurtful."

Buddhism – Udana-Varga 5:18

"In everything, do to others as you would have them do to you; for this is the law of the prophets."

Christianity – Jesus in Matthew 7:12

"One word which sums up the basis of all good conduct…

loving kindness. Do not do to others what you do not want done to yourself."

Confucianism – Confucius, Analects 15:23

"This is the sum of duty: do not do to others what would cause pain if done to you."

Hinduism – Mahabharata 5:15-17

"Not one of you truly believes until you wish for others what you wish for yourself."

Islam – The Prophet Muhammad, Hadith

"One should treat all creatures in the world as one would like to be treated."

Jainism – Mahavira, Sutrakritanga

"What is hateful to you, do not do to your neighbor, This is the whole Torah; all the rest is commentary."

Judaism – Hillel, Talmud, Shabbat 31a

"I am a stranger to no one; and no one is a stranger to me. Indeed, I am a friend to all."

Sikhism – Guru Granth Sahib

"Regard your neighbor's gain as your own gain, and your neighbor's loss as your own loss."

Taoism – T'ai Shang Kan Yin P'ien 213-218

"We affirm and promote respect for the interdependent web of all existence of which we are a part."

Unitarianism – Unitarian Principle

"An' harm none, do as thou wilt."

Wicca – The Wiccan Creed

"Do not do unto others whatever is injurious to yourself."

Zoroastrianism – Shayast-na-Shayast 13:29

"You shall not take vengeance, nor bear any grudge against the children of your people, but you shall love your neighbor as yourself: I am the LORD."

YHWH, Leviticus 19:18

"For all the law is fulfilled in one word, even in this; Thou shalt love thy neighbor as thyself."

Galatians 5:14

"This is the sum of duty; do naught onto others what you would not have them do unto you."

Hinduism - Mahabharata

Humanists affirm that individual and social problems can only be resolved by means of human reason, intelligent effort, critical thinking joined with compassion and a spirit of empathy for all living beings.

Humanism

"In happiness and suffering, in joy and grief, we should regard all creatures as we regard our own self."

Jainism - Lord Mahavir 24th Tirthankara

"Take heed to thyself, my child, in all thy works; and be discreet in all thy behavior. And what thou thyself hatest, do to no man."

Judaism - Tobit 4.14-15

"Do not wrong or hate your neighbor. For it is not he who you wrong, but yourself."

Native American - Pima proverb

Be charitable to all beings, love is the representative of
God.

Shintoism - Ko-ji-ki Hachiman Kasuga

"Do not create enmity with anyone as God is within everyone."

Sikhism - Guru Arjan Devji 259. Guru Granth Sahib

"To do as one would be done by, and to love one's neighbor
as one's self, constitute the ideal perfection of utilitarian
morality."

Utilitarianism - John Stuart Mill

"That nature alone is good which refrains from doing to
another whatsoever is not good for itself."

Zoroastrianism - Dadisten I dinik, 94,5

It is in this spirit that the Freemasonry looks to the idea
of a divine presence as a Great Architect of the Universe -
the planner of all things big and small. This identification
has several incarnations, but can perhaps be expressed in
a way of the ancient Romans under the figure of Sophia -
the source of wisdom who is matriarch of the three sisters

Faith, Hope, and Charity, which taken together form the embodiment of Love for one another. It is this love that Masonry has at its roots - a love of mankind in our brothers and sisters, for the society in which we exist, and the general well being of those around us.

Genesis 46:19-27 (KJV) reads:

19. The sons of Rachel, Jacob's wife, were Joseph and Benjamin. 20. And to Joseph in the land of Egypt were born Manasseh and Ephraim, whom Asenath, the daughter of Poti-Pherah priest of On, bore to him. 21. The sons of Benjamin were Belah, Becher, Ashbel, Gera, Naaman, Ehi, Rosh, Muppim, Huppim, and Ard. 22. These were the sons of Rachel, who were born to Jacob: fourteen persons in all. 23. The son of Dan was Hushim. 24. The sons of Naphtali were Jahzeel, Guni, Jezer, and Shillem. 25. These were the sons of Bilhah, whom Laban gave to Rachel his daughter, and she bore these to Jacob: seven persons in all. 26. All the persons who went with Jacob to Egypt, who came from his body, besides Jacob's sons' wives, were sixty-six persons in all. 27. And the sons of Joseph who were born to him in Egypt were two persons. All the persons of the house of Jacob who went to Egypt were seventy.

Acacia

Itself, a unique and sacred symbol of immortality and is emblematic to the progress of the soul. Fittingly, it is the mark of Hiram's resting place.

Genesis 49:9 (KJV) reads:

Judah is a lion's whelp; From the prey, my son, you have gone up. He bows down, he lies down as a lion; And as a lion, who shall rouse him?

Revelation 5:1-5 (NIV) reads:

1. Then I saw in the right hand of him who sat on the throne a scroll with writing on both sides and sealed with seven seals. 2. And I saw a mighty angel proclaiming in a loud voice, "Who is worthy to break the seals and open the scroll?" 3. But no one in heaven or on earth or under the earth could open the scroll or even look inside it. 4. I wept and wept because no one was found who was worthy to open the scroll or look inside. 5. Then one of the elders said to me, "Do not weep! See, the Lion of the tribe of Judah, the Root of David, has triumphed. He is able to open the scroll and its seven seals."

The Four Nines

The four nine cards include:

Nine of Swords: Cruelty (Mars in Gemini)

Nine of Cups: Happiness (Jupiter in Pisces)

Nine of Wands: Strength (Luna in Sagittarius)

Nine of Discs (Pentacles): Gain (Venus in Virgo)

Further, in the four nines, the nine of swords representing the battle with oneself — a battle which must be won. The nine of cups, or the wish card, that represents desire (the product of change). The nine of wands representing the strength of will to change; determination and energy. And, the nine of pentacles (discs) representing the product of change and prosperity — enjoying the fruits of their labor.

Ecclesiastes 12 (NIV)

1. Remember your Creator

in the days of your youth,

before the days trouble come

and the years approach when you will say,

"I find no pleasure in them"—

2. before the sun and the light

and the moon and the stars grow dark,

and the clouds return after the rain;

3. when the keepers of the house tremble,
   and the strong men stoop,

when the grinders cease because they are few,
   and those looking through the windows grow dim;

4. when the doors to the street are closed
   and the sound of grinding fades;

when people rise up at the sound of birds,
   but all their songs grow faint;

5. when people are afraid of heights
   and of dangers in the streets;

when the almond tree blossoms
   and the grasshopper drags itself along
   and desire no longer is stirred.

Then people go to their eternal home
   and mourners go about the streets.

6. Remember him—before the silver cord is severed,
   and the golden bowl is broken;

before the pitcher is shattered at the spring,
   and the wheel broken at the well,

7. and the dust returns to the ground it came from,
   and the spirit returns to God who gave it.

8. "Meaningless! Meaningless!" says the Teacher.

"*Everything is meaningless!*"

9. Not only was the Teacher wise, but he also imparted knowledge to the people. He pondered and searched out and set in order many proverbs. 10 The Teacher searched to find just the right words, and what he wrote was upright and true.

11. The words of the wise are like goads, their collected sayings like firmly embedded nails—given by one shepherd. 12. Be warned, my son, of anything in addition to them.

Of making many books there is no end, and much study wearies the body.

13. Now all has been heard;

   here is the conclusion of the matter:

Fear God and keep his commandments,

   for this is the duty of all mankind.

14. For God will bring every deed into judgment,

   including every hidden thing,

   whether it is good or evil.

FOOTNOTES

1. *The Golden Rule — see appendix*

2. Cirlot, Juan Eduardo. *A Dictionary of Symbols.* London: Routledge & Kegan Paul, 1978. Print.

3. *Ibid*

4. *Ibid*

5. *Ibid*

6. Schimmel, Annemarie. *The Mystery of Numbers.* New York: Oxford U, 1994. Print.

7. Trismegistus, Hermes, and Brian P. Copenhaver. *Hermetica: The Greek Corpus Hermeticum and the Latin Asclepius in a New English Translation, with Notes and Introduction by Brian P. Copenhaver.* Cambridge: Cambridge UP, 2002. Print.

8. Regardie, Israel. *A Garden of Pomegranates: Skrying on the Tree of Life*: Llewellyn, 2002. Print.

9. Trismegistus, Hermes, and Brian P. Copenhaver. *Hermetica: The Greek Corpus Hermeticum and the Latin Asclepius in a New English Translation, with Notes and Introduction by Brian P. Co-*

penhaver. Cambridge: Cambridge UP, 2002. Print.

10. Regardie, Israel. *A Garden of Pomegranates: Skrying on the Tree of Life.* Llewellyn, 2002. Print.

11. Kircher, Athanasius. *Oedipus Aegyptiacus*

12. Cirlot, Juan Eduardo. *A Dictionary of Symbols.* London: Routledge & Kegan Paul, 1978. Print.

13. Hall, Manly P. *Masonic Orders of Fraternity.* Los Angeles: Philosophical Research Society, 1978. Print.

14. Davidson, Charles. *Studies in the English Mystery Plays: A Thesis Presented to the Philosophical Faculty of Yale.* University (classic Reprint). S.l.: FORGOTTEN, 2016. Print.

15. *Ibid*

16. *Ibid*

17. *Ibid*

18. *Ibid*

19. *Ibid*

20. *Ibid*

21. Churton, Tobias. *Freemasonry: The Reality.* Addlestone: Lewis, 2009. Print.

22. *Ibid*

23. *Ibid*

24. *Ibid*

25. *Ibid*

26. *Third Degree Ritual*

27. *Scottish Rite Louisiana Degree* Ritual working under the Grand Lodge of Louisiana ritual, revised 1963.

28. *Ibid*

29. *Genesis 46:19-27 — see appendix*

30. *Ecclesiastes 12 — see appendix*

31. *Scottish Rite Louisiana Degree*

32. *The acacia — see appendix*

33. *Scottish Rite Louisiana Degree*

34. *Ibid*

35. Trismegistus, Hermes, and Brian P. Copenhaver. *Hermetica: The Greek Corpus Hermeticum and the Latin Asclepius in a New English Translation, with Notes and Introduction by Brian P. Copenhaver.* Cambridge: Cambridge UP, 2002. Print.

36. *Genesis 49:9 — see appendix*

37. *Revelation 5:1-5 — see appendix*

38. See The Apprentice - A Treatise on the First Degree of Freemasonry (2014) by the author.

39. Cirlot, Juan Eduardo. *A Dictionary of Symbols.* London: Routledge & Kegan Paul, 1978. Print.

40. Supreme Council or the Thirty-third Degree. *Morals and Dogma: The Ancient and Accepted Scottish Rite of Freemasonry.* Charleston: L.H. Jenkins, Inc, 1952. Print.

41. Ibid

42. *Ibid*

43. *Ibid*

44. *Ibid*

45. *Ibid*

46. Case, Paul Foster. Esoteric *Keys of Alchemy.* Vancouver: Ishtar, 2008. Print.

47. *The Sanskrit word for the aether or invisible*

48. Case, Paul Foster. *Esoteric Keys of Alchemy.* Vancouver: Ishtar, 2008. Print.

49. Supreme Council or the Thirty_third Degree. *Morals and Dogma: The Ancient and Accepted Scottish Rite of Freemasonry.* Charleston: L.H. Jenkins, Inc, 1952. Print.

50. *Ibid*

51. *Ibid*

52. *The four nine cards — see appendix*

53. "Tree of Life:Tarot." *Thelemapedia: The Encyclopedia of Thelema & Magick | Tree of Life:Tarot.* N.p., n.d. Web. Dec. 2016. <http://www.thelemapedia.org/index.php/Tarot_and_the_Tree_of_Life>.

54. Cirlot, Juan Eduardo. *A Dictionary of Symbols.* London: Routledge & Kegan Paul, 1978. Print.

55. Collins, Tom. "Mythic Reflections." Context Institute. N.p., Dec. 1985. Web. Dec. 2016. <http://www.context.org/iclib/ic12/campbell>.

56. Ibid

57. *"come absoluto, non ha che far con noi"* Eliade, Mircea. Myth and Reality. Harper & Row, 1987.

FOOTNOTES

INDEX

ABOUT THE AUTHOR

Gregory B. Stewart

A student of the Western Mystery tradition (Western Esotericism), Greg (Gregory) B. Stewart has explored the rites of initiation through a variety of initiatory systems with the express goal of understanding the deeper meaning behind them. In that process, Greg's exploration has converged with mainstream and esoteric religious traditions, rituals of religious practice and their intersecting undercurrents. Now, on the other side of that journey, the focus of his attention is on how those intersections relate to the *Great Work* — a subject he explores in his book series on the Symbolic Lodge.

As devoted student of the esoteric, Greg is a firm believer in the Masonic connection to the

Hermetic traditions of antiquity, its evolution through the ages and its present configuration as the antecedent to most present day currents of esoteric and occult practice. Called a masonic "bodhisattva," he is a self-styled searcher for that which was lost, a Hermetic Hermit and a believer in "what is above is so also below." You can read his occasional thoughts on the Hermetic tradition on the blog The Hermetic Circle.

Personally, Greg is an artist by nature and education. Professionally, his work spans a wide spectrum of communications, publishing and design. Under the Masonic tradition Greg began his career in 1994 participating in a variety of roles, lodges and organizations. Much of his early written work on Freemasonry can be found in his blog Masonic Traveler covering a period from 2005 to 2009. In 2008 Greg co-hosted and produced the Masonic Central podcast, with Dean Kennedy and went on to publish and produce FreemasonInformation.com as Masonic Traveler, alongside Fred Milliken, Tim Bryce and other Masonic notables.

www.ingramcontent.com/pod-product-compliance
Lightning Source LLC
Chambersburg PA
CBHW070818100426
42813CB00033B/3430/J